MY LIFE BEFORE AND ON HMS *JAMAICA*

MY LIFE BEFORE AND ON HMS *JAMAICA*

Denis Heckford

ARTHUR H. STOCKWELL LTD
Torrs Park   Ilfracombe   Devon
Established 1898
www.ahstockwell.co.uk

ISBN 978-0-7223-3985-5
Printed in Great Britain by
Arthur H. Stockwell Ltd
Torrs Park   Ilfracombe
Devon

COPYRIGHT ACKNOWLEDGEMENTS

Page 65: Article reproduced by kind permission of *The Sunday Times* of Malta, February 18, 1951, page 16. © Allied Newspapers Ltd, *www.timesofmalta.com*.

Page 68: West Herts Post & Watford Newspaper, Edition No 3820, 21 September 1950.

Page 70: Article reproduced by kind permission of the *Daily Express*, Express Newspapers, London.

There are instances where we have been unable to trace or contact the copyright holder.

Contents

CHAPTER 1: Schooldays

When I was about six years old I started at Blackhorse School. (I started late because of troubles with my nerves.) Well, on the way to school I often climbed an oak tree in Peanut Lane, as I loved climbing trees. There was a chestnut fence which I climbed to get into the branches of the oak tree. Well, one morning I suddenly realised I was late for school, and in my hurry to get down I slipped and fell. An acorn stuck right up my nose and I couldn't get the darn thing out. I had to walk to school with this thing sticking out of my nose, and when I arrived I was taken to see Nitty, the nit nurse. Nitty stuck a big needle into the acorn and extracted it, but my nose bled so much that I was sent home. When I got home I got a good clout for doing what I had done.

The following day at school, I was in the playground and a kid came up behind me and cut a chunk off the top of my middle finger, so there was hell to pay again. My mother thought I had been mucking about with glass, so I got another clout. Anyway the kid was punished and my mother took me away from that school and sent me to Chesham Bois School.

My eldest brother was already established there, so I just followed his example: whatever he did I did.

My brother and his mates had built a chicken coop and run in a small wood, and we filled it with stolen chickens. Every time we came home from school, we would take a sack down to the farm on Chestnut Lane and bring back a chicken. We never used to have breakfast at home; we used to get up very early, take some bread and go to the coop to collect some eggs, which we boiled on a fire in the wood. That went on for some time until my brother caught a fir tree alight when he was mucking about one day with a bit of lighted vine. The police were called and our chicken coop was discovered. We had to collect the chickens together, take them back to the farm, apologise to the farmer and accept our punishment. When the police officer asked us if we had harmed the chickens, I said no, but I told him my brother had got hold of a chicken and Stan Windsor had got hold of its head and they had twisted, but they couldn't hold it firmly enough to kill it. The police officer turned away and I could see that he was laughing; he thought it was quite funny.

I got let off, as I was only six, but my brother, who was two years older, had to go away and live with my aunt for a while. The funny thing about this incident is that our mother never questioned why we never wanted breakfast.

When I first started at Blackhorse School, I sometimes used to walk home with Bernard Beardmore, who lived close to where I lived at the time. One day, we had just come under the bridge, and we were walking past a horse chestnut tree when poor old Bernard was suddenly soaked. We looked up and saw a naked bloke up in the tree, peeing down on him. Luckily I was to one side, so it missed me.

When Bernard got home, his mother thought he had been playing about with water in the puddles, and she gave him a good hiding.

At another time, I went scrumping for pears, but unfortunately the owner saw me. He shouted, and I ran like the dickens the way I had gone in, but I tripped over an old, broken fence and ended up with a spike in my leg. There was no National Health Service then, and my parents couldn't afford to call a doctor even though muscle and sinews protruded from the hole in my leg. There was not too much blood, so mother pushed everything back in place, cleaned the wound properly and then put a bandage on with some kind of ointment. I still have quite a big scar, but on the whole the injury healed wonderfully well and I was soon able to walk long distances again – which I loved.

As you can see, I was rather a hardy kid, and I

used to get up to quite a lot of mischief. By the time I was about seven and a half I had lost all nervousness; I became in a way quite fearless; nothing seemed to bother me too much.

One day, Les Lancaster and myself thought we would play a practical joke on old Johnny Barker, our headmaster, who had a wooden leg and drove a motorbike and sidecar. Well, when lessons ended, while he was busy marking books, we managed to remove the cotter pin on his kick-start.

Les Lancaster and I were behind a bit of cover when he came out to start his motorbike, and we watched him jump up and come down heavily on the kick-start. Of course, with the cotter pin removed, it offered no resistance and he fell arse over head.

We thought it was very funny at the time, but the following day at school we didn't think it was quite so funny. He had found out who was responsible, so we had six of the best on each hand. It really was six of the best – he could really lay it on!

Not long after that, Les Lancaster and I went down to Amersham Fair. We had quite a good time and we managed to 'win' one or two things, in our own fashion. We walked home with them, fully loaded. Les had to go to Hyde Heath and I had to go the opposite way down Chestnut Lane to Weller Road in Amersham. It was quite a long walk, but Les was frightened to go on his own and so he asked me to go with him up the dark lane towards Hyde Heath.

When we got to where there were lights again he said he was OK to carry on home on his own, and I turned back down Chestnut Lane, which at that time was unlit. There were no houses, and it was just hedges and darkness on either side.

When I reached Weller Road, I saw my mother walking home, so I crossed over and crept alongside the hedge so that she wouldn't see me.

I reached home before she did, and my old father said, "Where on earth have you been?"

I just told him straight that we had been down to Amersham Fair, and I showed him the prizes that I had 'won', as I said, in my own fashion.

He said, "Never mind that! Quick – get upstairs before your mum gets back."

At the time I was sleeping in the same bed as my two brothers. Les slept on the outside, I slept in the middle, and Wilfred slept on the wall side. I hadn't realised what the time was: it was 1.30 in the morning.

When my mother came in, she dragged me out of bed, walloped me all the way down the stairs and all the way back up again, and slung me back in bed.

I understand now why she was so cross: she was worried sick because I had gone off on my own until 1.30 in the morning. As I said, I didn't seem to have any fear then, although I had started off in such a nervous manner when I was younger.

At Chesham Bois School, old Johnny Barker used

to love using the cane, so one day Les Lancaster and I broke his canes and stuck them up the chimney. When the fire was lit in the morning, the canes began to burn and the darn things fell down on to the fire.

Old Johnny Barker knew who the ringleaders were. He came out with new canes and again we received six of the best.

There was a boy, a couple of years older than myself, who was always bullying me. Well, one day he had a new bicycle with a nice lamp and pump, and when he went to the shops after school I followed him. While he was in a shop helping himself to sweets and what have you, I let his tyres down and nicked his pump and his lamp. Then I nipped across on to Amersham Common and dug a hole and buried them.

The boy knew who was responsible, so the police were called. I was walking home when the police car caught up with me. I told them I had taken the pump and lamp because the boy was bullying me, but I would never reveal where I hid them. My mother couldn't make me do it; the police couldn't make me do it. In the end everything quietened over, and that boy never ever bullied me again. That was another lesson I learned, and I think it taught him a lesson as well. It did a bit of good all round, I think.

I do not wish to brag, but these things actually happened. It wasn't what you might call clever stuff, but it made me feel better to know that I had got a little bit of my own back on somebody who was a bully. From then on, if I ever saw a boy bullying a younger lad, then I went and gave him a darn good clout – the bully, I mean. That has been my policy, more or less, throughout my life, even if the bullies were older than me or if I got a belting now and again. Anyhow, no matter how badly hurt I was they could never ever make me cry; and neither could my mother, when she gave me a good hiding. I just used to grin; and when, as a result, she hit me more, I would then pretend to cry. If I was scolded rather than hit, that used to make me well up more than anything else.

Of course, all our time wasn't spent in getting into mischief. Like all other kids, we had our games, and one of our favourite games was spinning tops. There was a nice, smooth tarmacadam road, the White Lion Road, up at Amersham and we used to spin our tops from the White Lion pub to the Blackhorse Bridge and then back again. It was roughly half a mile each way, and we used to spin our tops up and down, up and down. Children of today, and even a lot of grown-ups today, do not realise how little traffic there was in those days. Occasionally a car or a lorry would come along, and then we would leave our tops spinning in the road and just hope that they wouldn't be run over. It was very seldom that we got a smashed top. If we did, we just went into the local shop and bought another one for a couple of coppers – about tuppence.

We also used to make our own four-wheel trolleys and race them down hills. Naturally we always had cuts and bruises, but that was a part of our life in those days.

We would walk home along Stubbs Wood from Chesham Bois School, and, as we passed a particular house, a parrot would scream at us from its perch near a garage at the far end of the long drive. There was a hosepipe and tap nearby, which the owner used to wash his car. Well, one day, when I was with a group of friends, including my brothers and Tom Seymour, I turned on the tap and gave the parrot a darn good sprinkling with the hose. It screamed its head off something terrible! The bloke came running out and we all ran off. I believe that man waited for us day after day, but we cut round another way and avoided him.

One day, Billy and Mary Wright, a pair of twins who were not part of our group, were walking past the man's house when he rushed out and caught hold of them. Although they were entirely blameless he gave them a good hiding for what I had done. After that he never waited for us any more, so we were able to walk past his house again. I wasn't very proud of the fact that others had taken the punishment for something I had done, but I consoled myself with the thought that at least I had got away with it.

Our behaviour wasn't all bad. On one occasion a poor little old lady in the Grey Cottages at Amersham asked us to join her and say prayers for her little cat, which had just died. She thought our prayers would help to send it on its way to heaven, so we did our best to oblige her. It made her quite happy, you see.

We weren't always on the naughty side, but it was hard sometimes for people to see the good in us. Sometimes only the rough edges showed.

When we were in the Grey Cottages and I was about six and a half years old, I once overheard my mother talking to Betty Rickards, a young friend of hers.

Betty Rickards said, "Let me know which one of your boys behaves best, and I will take him to see *Snow White and the Seven Dwarfs* on Saturday."

Guess who turned out to be the best behaved boy of the week?

Betty Rickards asked my mother, "Well, Mrs Heckford, who was the best lad?"

My mother replied, "Well, I hate to say this, Betty, but Den has been a little angel all this week, so it will be him you will be taking to see *Snow White and the Seven Dwarfs*."

So Betty took me to see the film, and we had popcorn and goodness knows what. After that, I reverted back to the little toad I really was. Sorry – not toad, but the little devil I really was!

One day, after a game with some mates, I started

to walk home and suddenly the sky became a deep, deep red. I pointed it out to a passer-by, and he, being rather funny, just turned around and said, "Oh, the world is on fire." It was the reddest sky I had ever seen. I ran home and told my parents, but, as I was late home, I was given a clout and told not to be such a silly boy. Apparently it was the aurora borealis, or northern lights. The sky was completely red. There was no blue or any other colour at all, except red. At first it was frightening, but, when I got used to seeing it, it was one of the most amazing things I have ever seen in my whole life.

CHAPTER 2: On the Farm

When my father got a job on a farm, looking after the dairy herd, my brother Leslie and I had to help with the milking, and that meant being up at 5.30 every morning, summer or winter. My job was to go and fetch the cows; Leslie's job was to help my father get the mangers ready with the food (the maize, the chaff and the cow nuts, etc.)

I used to go down across the fields, calling the cows by their names. I won't repeat their names, as there were too many of them, but they were all named after flowers. Anyway, they would come to me and then, as I walked back across the fields, they would follow me up to the milking shed. That was the beginning of my day. It was quite a busy life, but I really enjoyed it.

My parents had grown up on farms, and so they knew exactly what they were doing. When it came to the milking, Dad taught us what to do. It didn't take us long to learn – about one day was all it took. By the second day, Leslie and I were quite proficient at milking.

Mum used to go out with old Mr Martin, the owner, delivering the milk, the butter and the eggs.

The cows all had their own stalls and they knew exactly which stall to go to for their food and to have the chains put around their necks while we milked them. However, there was one awkward cow. She was the only one that was not named after a flower. She was called Red. I was never allowed to go near her because she used to lash out with her hoofs and she had a terrific kick. Les and my father had to tie her back legs so that she couldn't kick, and then one would hold her while the other one did the milking. She was always the awkward one. She would go into one of the other cows' stalls and they always had to back her out and get her into her own. However, she used to give a generous amount of milk. I think that was the reason why Mr Martin kept her on.

The animals always used to be fed very well, and they were very contented cows. Whilst they were feeding, they relaxed and let the milk flow freely.

Now and again my brother and I used to have a little skylark. My father would be on one stool milking one cow, I would be in the middle milking another one, and Les would be on the third one. Suddenly I would feel a warm splash at the back of my neck and ear, and of course Les had just directed the teat at me and gave me a squirt. When he went back to milking, and was concentrating on that, I would retaliate and try to catch him in the face. We used to have a little bit of fun now and again, as you can imagine.

Once the milking was finished, we would release the cows back into the pastures, and then my brother and I had one more job before we got ready for school. The chickens laid eggs everywhere – in the barns and in the hedgerows – and we all had to share the job of collecting the eggs. We learnt to tell the difference between a good egg, a bad egg and an egg with a young chick inside. We were taught to tell the difference by holding each end of the egg to our lips. If it was warm at only one end, it was a good egg; if it was cold at both ends, it was bad; but if it was warm at both ends, it meant there was a young chick inside. That was the only method we had in those days. We didn't have all the complicated gear they have today.

Whilst we were at school, my father had the job of cleaning out the mangers in the cowsheds and getting everything ready again for the evening milking. It was quite a busy and hectic life, but I thoroughly enjoyed it.

All the water we used on the farm had to be drawn from the well. There was no such thing as running water in taps, so you can imagine the job my father had cleaning the cowsheds out. The water had to be boiled before it was drinkable, but in fact it tasted far better than anything you will get out of the taps today.

Despite the amount of water we used, the level

of water in the well stayed constant. It was always three parts full, ready to be drawn. We never had any shortage of water whatsoever. Sometimes when we drew the bucket up there might be a frog or two in the water, but we were told to throw them back because they helped to purify the water. Whether that is true or not I do not know, but we always used to do it.

When we came home from school, the first thing we did was change from our school clothes. Then we did the milking. After that we had our tea and then we went back into the dairy, where the milk that hadn't been sold during the day was poured from the churns into a big container at the top of the separator. One of us would turn a handle to separate the cream from the milk, and this was quite a tiring job.

The most enjoyable task came at the end, when the machine had to be cleaned. I think there were twenty small metal cone-shaped cups, which fitted down the stem of the machine and we used to squabble just slightly over who would have the pick of them. The cream tasted absolutely delicious to us kids.

When we had eaten what we could, Mrs Martin used to bring a big pot of water to clean and sterilise all the machine parts. Everything in the dairy had to be kept clean.

That was the daily routine.

There were three horses on the farm. Two were

big carthorses – shires – and I don't know what the other one was. Charlie was the largest, Blossom was not quite as big, and Peggy, was a bit smaller still. Leslie always used to have Charlie, I always used to have Blossom, and Wilfred (if he felt like getting up) had Peggy. There were no saddles, no blankets and no reins. We had to climb on their backs and hold on to their manes – and, believe me, we had to hold on quite firmly. We were only kids, so our legs never went round them at all – they just stuck out over the sides. Then we used to gallop across the fields.

Just imagine: a big cart horse galloping across a field with a youngster on its back bouncing up and down! It was quite funny really, and the ride was most enjoyable – until one day I slipped. I went round underneath the horse and dropped to the ground. It happened very quickly, but that horse realised straight away; it must have, because it kicked up its hind legs to clear right over me. It was absolutely amazing!

It could have been very serious, but I was undaunted. As soon as the horse stopped, I climbed back up and away we went again. We were hardy kids, there is no doubt about it. And it was very, very enjoyable.

Some of the cream from the dairy was made into butter. It was put into a butter churn, and the churn was turned regularly until the butter formed. When it was ready, it would clump about in the churn, and then Mrs Martin would take it out, divide it up and pat it into shape using a big butter board and butter pats. She was never far out on the weight. She would flop each pat of butter on to some greaseproof butter paper on the scales, and then she would wrap it up. It was very remarkable how accurate she was in measuring out that butter.

There was a nice big pond near the farmhouse, and we used to get moorhens nesting there. We used to paddle out, right up to our kneecaps, in order to collect eggs from their nests. We used to take two from each nest. The moorhens would then lay more eggs. Because they were so small, we used to fry eight or nine of them in the pan at once, and Leslie and I would have them for our breakfast or our tea.

We were quite versatile kids: we could more or less do anything. We didn't have to rely on our parents to cook our meals, because we could help ourselves in that respect. We used to enjoy those little eggs. They were very tasty. When the moorhens stopped replenishing the missing eggs, we left them alone so that they could hatch their chicks, which they used to do quite successfully.

Life on the farm was quite a rugged life, and of course it was very, very close to nature all the time. In fact, townspeople would think it was pretty raw and pretty rough. It was good honest, natural nature.

When a cow is bulling it means she is jumping

on other cows, and it indicates that she needs a bull. When that happened, my father would put the cow in the bull ring. The bull ring was directly outside our living room window. One day, Leslie and I were kneeling on the settee watching progress from the window. Suddenly the bull hopped up on the cow, and Leslie nudged me and said, "Look, Den, look – it's ready, it's ready, it's ready!" In our eagerness to see what was happening, our heads crashed together with a heavy smack, and at that moment our father came into the room, so we never did see what happened.

We had three dogs on the farm: an old English sheepdog, a greyhound and a terrier. They were brilliant rat-catchers. Every farm has rats and mice and ours was no exception. The cats used to attend to the mice and the dogs used to attend to the rats. You very seldom saw a rat or a mouse around the farm, because those animals were great at their work.

The dogs and cats were not allowed in the dairy or the residential part of the farm at all. They slept in the barns and sheds. They were friendly dogs – there was nothing vicious about them towards us – but if they saw a rat, boy! There was no stopping them. They were absolutely brilliant.

There was a wood adjacent to the fields, and in the wood there was a rabbit warren. Sometimes we put nets over the rabbit holes, and the dogs would chase the rabbits into the nets, where they became entangled. Then we would have a good rabbit pie – and boy! you couldn't get anything better.

A group of gypsies used to come to the farm about every three or four months. They would stay in the bottom field for a couple of nights, and Les and I would go down and sit and listen to their yarns and have a little bit of fun with their kids. (In the normal way we had no other kids to play with on the farm.)

One night we asked Mum if we could sleep with the gypsies for the night, and she gave us the all-clear so down we went. They were real Romany gypsies, and they were wonderfully clean people. Naturally, they used to do a little bit of poaching and so we enjoyed a meal of rabbit pie and sat around the campfire listening to their yarns. We slept rough under the caravan, and it was a wonderful experience. It was a beautiful caravan – horse-drawn, naturally – and it was wonderfully clean inside. All the brass was gleaming, and everything was spotless.

When they departed, there was no sign that they had been there at all, apart from where the fire had been and where hazel branches had been cut from hedges to make pegs. They used to sell the pegs from door to door.

The so-called gypsies or travellers of today leave an awful lot of rubbish wherever they go – they never seem to clean up behind them at all – whereas the old Romany gypsies always left the place more or less as they found it. They were great people.

My brother and I always looked forward to their next visit. We only stayed with them that one night, but whenever they came back we always went down to see them. It was just wonderful to see them every time they came.

A sad thing happened on the farm one morning. When my brother went to get the cows, he found Peggy, the smallest horse, dead. Her throat had been slashed from her forelegs right up to under her chin. At first we thought it had been done by some vicious person, but, a couple of days later, Blossom was found in a similar plight. She was still on her feet, but her chest was open from just above her forelegs to below her chin. We realised then that Mr Martin had put the bull into the field, and the bull had gored the horses. Poor old Blossom!

The vet cleaned the wound and stitched it up, and Leslie and I had to take turns, for a couple of hours at a time, to waft the flies off her wound. We sat up with her until darkness fell and the flies left her alone. Luckily, this was holiday time for us kids. Early every morning, for about ten days, Leslie or I would sit there wafting the flies away from her chest to keep her wound clean and clear. We were happy to do all we could to help her to recover, and we were delighted when she pulled through. She was such a lovely horse. We all loved her.

While Blossom was recuperating, poor old Charlie had to draw the cart. The milk float was too small for him, so he had to pull the larger cart.

It used to take them longer to deliver the milk, butter and eggs, because he hadn't got the pace of Blossom.

Not long after this, Mr Martin got pneumonia and died. Mrs Martin couldn't run the farm, so she sold it. The new people took it over, and we were booted out. We were no longer required. I don't know what happened to the horses or the farm, or the cattle.

CHAPTER 3: The Outbreak of War

My father got another job straight away, and we moved to a cottage on a farm on Whelpley Hill. Unfortunately, Leslie decided to convert the top of the woodshed into a pigeon loft without telling the farmer, and as a result my father was sacked.

We moved into a great big farmhouse with fields on three sides. On the other side was a wood. It seemed very eerie to us kids, but by then I was nearly eleven and I was quite fearless.

The war had just started and my father enlisted in the forces, although because he was nearly forty he didn't have to do it. He enlisted in order to ensure that we would have money.

Well, one night, with my father away, an idiot of a man came round, making noises. My brothers and sister were pretty terrified by the noise he was making. I went to the door and lowered my voice as much as I possibly could and shouted at him. It was a chap who used to live next door to us when we were on the farm on Whelpley Hill and he was trying to give us a fright. He came and apologised the next day and said what a "brave little sod" I was for shouting at him to go away.

When the war started, we were at Ashley Green school. Hour after hour after hour, Bren-gun carriers, tanks, lorries and other military vehicles streamed past our school. I shall never forget it. There were too many to count and they were all going in the direction of Aylesbury. They were still trundling by when we were in the class in the afternoon, and when we went home there were still some coming. Lord knows where they came from! They were all British, because at that time the Americans weren't even contemplating coming over to this country. Later we realised that they must have been part of the expeditionary force which was sent over to France.

My father became a sapper in the Royal Engineers and he ended up in France too, building bridges over rivers and suchlike. Later, when the British were being driven back by the Germans, his job was to blow bridges up, and to destroy other buildings in order to reduce the threat from snipers.

My father was one of the lucky ones. He was one of the last to get to Dunkirk, but he was evacuated with the other 300,000 British soldiers.

Not long after all the military vehicles went past the school, my mother got a flat in Chorleywood, and we lived there all through the war.

In the winter of 1939/40 the snow was up to our hips, and it was above my mother's knees. She couldn't get down to the road to go and get some shopping, so the postman, who had big rubber leggings to protect him from the snow, piggybacked her down to the road, from where she could walk up to the village. That was a comical thing to see, it really was!

There were no tractors or snowploughs available for clearing the roads and paths, so everything had to be done by hand. My eldest brother and I got shovels and we shovelled all the way across the field and down the drive so that when my mother came back she was able to walk up to the farmhouse. It was very, very hard work, but we did it, made fun of it and enjoyed it. I am afraid the kids of today just haven't got a clue when it comes to things like that.

Our old farmhouse was huge, and all the rooms were huge too. I think it was an old grange. The kitchen had two great big black cooking ranges in it. There were many bedrooms, but we were not allowed upstairs so we could not use them. We had to stay downstairs. There was a huge cellar underneath, which had been used for storing wine, but the remaining bottles were now empty. There were some very, very odd-shaped bottles down there; some were even in a kind of wickerwork holder.

It was very creepy down in the cellar – in fact, it was a very creepy house altogether – but it never bothered me one iota.

I had lived in eleven different houses by the time I was eleven years old, and I remember them all except the first one. One of them was a wooden bungalow which belonged to a farm my father worked on at that time. One morning he couldn't get the fire to light, so he poured some paraffin on the fire, and the result was that we hadn't got a home. The whole bungalow went up.

After that we lived in a train carriage, which was on blocks in a field on the same farm.

Then we moved to the old Grey Cottages in Amersham.

In Chorleywood, we had an upstairs flat. Mrs Southam's family had a flat in the bottom half of the building. Les went to the Chorleywood church school, on the other side of the common, about a mile away. I went to the Mill End senior school, roughly three miles away. They would not let me go to the Chorleywood church school, but I have never understood why not.

Anyway, the three-mile walk didn't daunt me, even on top of all the other things I had to do. I was now the chief cook and bottle-washer for the family of kids, because my mother was now working in an ammunition factory. Every morning I had to get up early, and I had to walk roughly three-quarters of a mile to Baldwin's, the baker's, to get two loaves of bread. I got to know the baker very well. His name was Mr Ryder. A very nice chap he was. Then I had to get back, prepare the breakfast and get Wilfred, Dorry and Brian off to school. Then I had three miles to walk to school – and I always arrived on time! That wasn't too bad, was it?

I was a quite a healthy lad, so it didn't bother me too much, but it is odd that I had to walk all that distance to school while my eldest brother only had to walk across the common. Things like this happened to me throughout my life.

After school, I had to get home and then get the kids their tea, and make sure there was something for my mother to eat when she got home. If there wasn't, then for poor old me there was hell to pay. I used to grin and make light of it. Leslie didn't do a thing; it was all left to me.

Sometimes my mother arranged for Mrs Southam to come up and give us our tea when we got home in the evening, and so there were times when I didn't have to do it.

At weekends, I used to cook the breakfasts, wash up, and then cook the dinners. Sometimes I would make a rabbit stew, or I would make an Irish stew from a scrag end of lamb. That was the kind of meal I used to prepare. It made me quite a handy bloke in the kitchen, and I became adept at cooking.

Sometimes we used to catch our own rabbits, and I would gut them and skin them. If my mother was inclined to do it, we would have a rabbit pie at the weekend, which was very good.

Quite a lot of the women worked in the

ammunition factory during the day, and they often went out for a good time together in the evenings. Everyone was trying to make the best of their situations.

It wasn't all doom and gloom for me – don't get me wrong. Thanks to Mrs Southam, I sometimes had great fun with the other kids. We used to make our own fun in those days, and some of it was a bit dodgy, but it was well worth the effort that we used to put into it. I used to enjoy my life; no matter what I had to do, I still used to enjoy it. It annoyed me sometimes that all the other kids were being looked after, while I was having to do a lot of the looking-after, but it didn't wear me out at all. I think it made me quite a resilient person in the end.

One day, after a couple of days of heavy snowfall, the snow was right up to my knees as I walked the three miles to school. As I went down Shepherds Lane to the school, I walked in the middle of the road, rolling a huge snowball. When it became so big that I could barely push it, I left it in the middle of the road and started again. By the time I got to the school, there must have been six huge snowballs in the middle of the road. (There wasn't a lot of traffic in those days, so it didn't matter too much.)

When I arrived, it was eleven o'clock, but the teacher said I was a brave lad to walk all that distance in the snow and she sent two girls down to the sweet shop to get me some sweets. I had to laugh because it was nothing at all to do with being brave. I had had some fun rolling those snowballs on the way to the school.

By the time I went home that night, all the snowballs had been pushed to the side of the road, and I could see tracks where a lorry had passed. I assume it was the coal lorry. I decided to be a good boy for a change, and I didn't do it again.

There was a trick we used to do with a nail and a key. We put a hollow key on one end of a string and a nail on the other end. Then we filled the hollow of the key with the match heads from Swan Vesta matches and pushed the nail into them. When the string was swung in an arc so that the nail hit against a wall, the result was quite a big, sharp bang.

Well, one day, during playtime at school, I filled a nice, big, hollow key with the heads of Swan Vesta matches and pushed my nail down tight on to the top of the matches. Through a window I could see three teachers with their cups in their hands. I gave an almighty swing with my nail and key, and there was a terrific bang! It was incredible! It blew the key to pieces. The three teachers were so startled that they dropped their cups of tea.

They knew I was the culprit because I had got lacerations all over my face and hands where the key had exploded and all the bits had hit me. I was lucky, I suppose, not to have injured my eyes.

I was sent to Mr Whitehead, the headmaster, and

he gave me a hell of a caning, but I took it all in my stride. I had done a naughty prank, so I had to pay for it.

In this day and age, schoolchildren bash people up and steal from them, but it wasn't like that with us. We used to do things like the trick with the nail and key, and we only hurt ourselves – well, the teachers lost their cups of tea, didn't they? It was quite a funny sight to see them standing there looking bewildered, with their cups and saucers on the floor.

At Mill End senior school, the boys never played with the girls; we had separate playgrounds and we sometimes had separate lessons. I was intrigued by the typewriters the girls used, and one day when they had gone out to play, I decided to have a look at one for myself. I went into the classroom and tapped away on the keys for a short time. Then I thought, 'Let's see what makes it work, then.' I pushed a pencil in the back of the machine, and I touched the ribbon with the pencil to see what would happen. Suddenly the spool flipped off and the ribbon entangled, and it seemed as though all the keys went flying everywhere. It wasn't vandalism; it was just that I was curious to see how the typewriter worked. Well, I didn't discover how it worked; instead I had to bend over a desk while Mr Whitehead took off his belt and belted me across the backside. He gave me up to about eight strokes – and boy, did that hurt! Nevertheless, it didn't deter me – I still had one or two more things up my sleeve.

One afternoon in September, we went across the railway and climbed a big fence to go scrumping in someone's back garden. There were some lovely red eating apples. We had had one or two before when we thought the owner was out. This time, however, he surprised us. There was a hell of a shout and we all ran, but my shirt front was loaded with apples and I couldn't run quite as quickly as the others. I got over the fence and was running up the bank to the railway when suddenly there was a bang and I felt something strike the heel of my boot. I reckon the chap had opened up with a .22 rifle. I doubt if he meant to hit me but we didn't go back into his garden any more after that.

About three days later, we went to his house to apologise. I showed him the heel of my boot, and he said, "I am terribly sorry. I didn't mean to be that close." Then he said, "I'll tell you what: you can pick as many apples as you like. Please, if ever you want any more, just come and ask."

Of course, this took away the excitement of scrumping, so we didn't bother.

In the light evenings we used to have to earn some money to pay for our shoes and our boots, because our mothers could never afford them. I got a job up on Catlips Farm. The farmer's name was Mr Cadman. He lost two of his sons at the beginning of the war. They were both in the RAF, and they were both killed in the Battle of Britain.

He was quite an unusual person. There was a rumour that he had been a slave driver in South Africa, which I can well believe because he used to drive us pretty hard – but he used to pay us, so that was OK.

One day we were storing silage in a silo. We were putting in alternate layers of cut grass and molasses. Every so often we had to go round and round, trampling it down. Mr Cadman was in front of me and the other two, Derek (known as Kip) and Freddie, were behind me. (Freddie and Kip were brothers.) I was directly behind Mr Cadman, and my head was just a little bit higher than his backside, and all the time, as he trotted around in front of me, he was farting. I was getting the full benefit of it, and I couldn't say anything. Kip kept digging me in the back to try to make me laugh, and I was trying not to do so.

Mr Cadman had two daughters called Evelyn and Jane. They both had horses. Evelyn had a beautiful big stallion. Well, one day we were walking home across the fields, and Kip, who was a bit of a devil, picked up a lump of turf and threw it at Evelyn's stallion. The stallion came charging at us, and we had to run for it.

Unfortunately, I had big heavy boots on; they had plimsolls, so they were across the field and over the gate while I lagged behind. The horse was gaining on me, so I suddenly swung round, put up my fists and said, "Come on, you brute!"

The stallion stopped dead and looked at me. I then turned round and ran, and I just made it to the gate before he caught up with me.

There was a spinney at the bottom of one of Mr Cadman's fields, and we made a camp there. We just used to muck around – firing catapults, and things like that. On one occasion, when we were going home, Kip heaved a big round boulder down the bank, straight through the side of our camp in the spinney. Unbeknown to us, Freddie was in there, and the boulder knocked him out.

We didn't know what to do, so we carried him back up to the farm. By the time we got there, he was just about coming round, and old Mr Cadman asked what had happened.

When we told him, he said, "That'll teach you to muck about on my property when you are supposed to be going home."

Anyway, he and his wife cleaned Freddie up and bandaged his head. (His wife was a really lovely person.)

When we got Freddie home, poor old Kip had to go through it! My mother used to give me the broom handle or the chair, or anything like that, across my back, but his mother had a high-heeled shoe which she kept handy. As he walked through the door, she gave him a couple of wallops with this shoe, right in his back. Boy that must have hurt! Well, it made him bawl. However, neither he nor Freddie were any the worse for their experience that day.

We used to buy a kind of granule called carbide, which produces gas when you put it in water. We used it to light our bicycle lamps in the old days. We would buy it from an old bicycle shop in Rickmansworth. Sometimes we would put some carbide granules in a treacle tin and hammer the lid down tight, and then we would go back about thirty paces and fire at it with our catapults. When one of us hit the tin, it would explode and the lid would go flying way up in the air.

One day, we tried the same thing with an old quart beer bottle. We put about two inches of water in the bottom with quite a bit of carbide, and screwed the air-tight top down very, very tightly.

I don't know which one of us hit it, but it went off with an almighty bang. If we hadn't been lying down, we might have been badly injured by the flying glass. However, some Italian prisoners of war were unloading coal nearby, and one of the guards came over to us and said, "Please don't do that any more – you have injured one of our prisoners." (He wasn't quite as polite as that.) The cork had hit one of the prisoners on the side of his head. They weren't very happy with us, so that put the kibosh on that pastime; we didn't do it any more.

After we had finished with this kind of lark, we always picked up the broken glass. Dogs were allowed to roam anywhere in those days, and we didn't want them to tread on the broken glass and cut their paws, so we used to pick up all the glass particles so that nothing could harm them or any other animals. That is how careful we were.

In Chorleywood they had a very old-fashioned fire engine. It had solid tyres and a top speed of about twenty-five miles an hour. If there was a fire on the common, it used to come round the same way: over the railway bridge and then sharp left. It took them ages to get around the corner, so when they got there we could jump on and go with them to help put out the fire. From time to time, we set a little fire going; then we used to go across with them on the fire engine and help put it out. Sometimes, instead of helping, we would spread it just a little bit more to add to the fun. However, we never made any serious fires; we always set light to patches that could be easily controlled. In fact, it used to do a bit of good, because when the gorse grew back it grew stronger. Sadly, there is hardly any gorse at all on the common now. They deliberately burned it down and then trees took over. At one time, you could see the church spire from any part of Chorleywood Common. Nowadays, because of the trees, you cannot see the spire until you are up near to the church.

During the war, lots of evacuees came to our school. They were so backward that we had to go over everything we had already learned, just so that they could catch up with us. It was so boring. One day I finished my arithmetic very early, and I was amusing myself by copying a picture of an

Aberdeen Angus bull into my book. When the teacher saw me drawing this bull, she gave me a clump around the ear – and it was quite a solid clump. I said that I had already done my arithmetic, and she said, "Well, it can't be very correct if you've done it so quickly, can it?"

I said, "I think it is. I have been over it twice."

Anyway, she looked at it and she said, "Oh yes! I am very sorry, Denis. I should not have smacked you. Carry on drawing."

From then on, whenever I finished ahead of the class I used to carry on with my drawing of this bull. When I had finished it, having also got my lessons right, the teacher held it up for all the class to see. She said she could hardly see the difference between the bull that I had copied and the bull in the book. I was so very, very proud of it, but I never ever bothered to do any more drawing after that.

Because I found it so easy, I became bored with school so I just did not bother to go. I just played truant every day for almost the whole year. My mother got a fine, which she couldn't pay, and I got a hiding, but I never ever went back to that school until the last six weeks of the year.

Instead of going to school, I would walk, walk and walk everywhere. I went bird's-nesting, and as long as I only collected one egg from each nest I felt it did no harm. On one occasion, I even shinned up a beech tree for a rook's egg. Rooks often build in the topmost branches of beech trees, so I shinned until I got to the branches, and then I went right to the top. I put the egg in my mouth and began to descend, but on the way down the parent birds attacked me and the egg broke in my mouth. I had to spit it out, but I was undeterred: I went straight back up and got another one. The rooks didn't touch me the second time; they let me go down without any bother at all. I suppose they must have thought, 'Well, if we keep doing that, he will keep coming up and we won't have any eggs left.' Anyway, I got down with my rook's egg intact.

Magpies' eggs are also very, very difficult to get because they always seem to build their nests in the biggest hawthorns. You cannot get to the nest without being scratched. However, I still got away with one of their eggs without too much trouble.

We saw quite a bit of the Battle of Britain from Chorleywood. We could see the planes towards London, and sometimes we saw them at night too. We had a lovely summer that year, and the sky was so clear and beautiful. Sometimes the planes even came overhead, and we used to stand there and watch them. From the common we could see the bombs landing on London, and all the way down to Chorleywood we could see in the distance the glow of the fires. The shells from the anti-aircraft guns would go straight up in a big barrage of perhaps thirty or forty in a group, and they all seemed to explode together, like fireworks, in what we called the 'flaming onions'.

A Wellington bomber, on its way back from a raid over France or Germany, crash-landed in a field at the bottom of Long Lane, and narrowly missed some big barns. The crew didn't even know they were in England. They were pretty well shook up, but none of them were injured.

On another occasion, a Spitfire crash-landed in a potato field. The pilot was a bit disorientated, and when some of us ran over towards him he started throwing the spuds that he had ploughed up with his plane. He only stopped when he realised we were shouting in English. We got shooed away by the military police.

One night an engine fell off a Lancaster bomber, which had been pretty badly shot up, and it fell through the roof of Alf Craft's house in Sarratt. The rest of the plane crashed into the sports field behind his house. Again, nobody was injured.

CHAPTER 4: Starting Work

By 1942, I had left school and I had to start work. I still had to look after the other kids because my mother was still in the ammunition factory.

I started at the local factory and I was always getting into trouble, even there. The other kids always seemed to want to fight me. Don't ask me why – perhaps it's because I got the better of them. One day, Stan Parrott, who was a lot bigger than I was, gave me a shove, so I grabbed hold of him and we began to fight. I was holding him on the floor when old George Bast, the foreman, came along and hit me on the head with the handle of a hammer.

"Come on, Heckford!" he said. "Get off him."

I just jumped up and, without thinking – it was automatic – I swung round and hit out. He went down like a log. They couldn't sack you in those days. You couldn't be sacked and you couldn't leave unless you moved from the district. Anyway, they suspended me for three days.

I had some funny, old, wooden-shafted golf clubs – all odds and ends they were really – and on one of those three days I took them up to Chorleywood Common. I had never played golf in my life before – I was just trying to hit the ball. Harry Darvell, who was one of the governors of the factory, spotted me and wanted to know why I wasn't at work.

I said, "I decked the foreman, so they suspended me for three days."

"Oh well," he said, "you had better have a game of golf with me."

After about twenty shots on one hole, he said, "Well, I think we have had enough for today, don't you?"

I think he had been hoping for a more challenging opponent.

While I was at the factory we used to have to do fire-watching when there was an air raid. We kids were light and nimble, so we had to get up on to the asbestos roof with some old binoculars and look for fires caused by incendiary bombs. This was quite a bit of fun really, because we had the binoculars and we could have a good look around. On one occasion an incendiary bomb set a hay rick on fire, so of course the old fire engine was called out for that, but we didn't see much else.

One lunchtime I was walking through the yard when a woman asked me if I could lift a box of bearings or nails (I forget which it was) on to a conveyor.

As I was a good lad, I said, "Yes, OK, I will do that."

However, as soon as I was inside the building I was grabbed by seven or eight women. They laid me on the conveyor and a big, horrible woman sat on my chest astride me. She stank. It was absolutely horrible. While she held me down, the others mucked about with me until I ejaculated, and then they called me a dirty young sod. While I had an erection, they stuck ball bearings down inside. They said they put in seven, but only six came out. Then they put some newspaper over me with my dick poking through, and they sent me along the conveyor to old Waggle, the paint sprayer. He sprayed me with a horrible, brown, low-leaded paint, and I had a hell of a job cleaning up afterwards.

This is one of the most disgusting things that has ever happened to me. It put me off women and girls for quite a long, long time. There was nothing I could do about it, so I just put up with it. It was no good telling anybody, because in those days that kind of thing was taken for granted.

In those days we left school at the age of fourteen, and we had to work the same hours as the men. We were treated as men, although we were only children really.

At the factory they had swing saws, cross-cut saws, circular saws, band saws – all types of saws. One day the chap who used to work the swing saw didn't realise that his thumb was in line with the saw. When he pressed the pedal, the swing saw came forward to cut the wood, and it took his thumb off at the same time.

When the bigwigs came from the Ministry to find out exactly what had happened, the chap who had been operating the saw with the injured man gave a demonstration. He held the wood in exactly the same place as the chap who had had his thumb cut off, and he pressed the pedal. The saw came forward and he lost his thumb as well.

It is quite ridiculous, but it is absolutely true.

After that, they put a guard on to the machine so it was impossible for the operator's fingers to get into the saw.

In the metalworks side of the factory we had to use a gas gun to remove all the solder from the returned metal ammunition boxes, so that they could be reused. The solder was used to seal the ammunition boxes. One night, somebody broke the nozzle from my igniter. He soldered it back on, but he didn't do the job properly. When I reached up to light my gun the next morning, the force of the gas knocked the nozzle off and a whole gush of gas hit me in the face and head. For a long, long time I wore a cap to cover the place where it had burnt the hair off my head. I had no eyebrows either.

It was quite frightening, but it didn't worry me too much.

After this, I was made an apprentice plumber with Albert Dowse and Dick Warner. From then on I didn't have to go into the factory any more; I didn't have to go near those stinking women.

One day I was going down into Loudwater with Albert Dowse when there was a big explosion from a transformer only about 150 yards away. (A transformer is one of the big, green, electric boxes you used to see on the side of the road.) Two men had been working on it with a welding torch and when we got down there, we saw that one of the men had been badly burnt. I have smelled burning flesh several times in my life, and it is a terrible smell.

Albert Dowse said, "Carry on, boy. Go to the house we were going to, and tell the lady to call an ambulance and the police." He didn't want me to go near the injured man, so he sent me to the house, which was only about 100 yards away.

Old Dick Warner was a very big man. He stood about six foot six and he was a real barrel of a man.

One day he showed me how to make a grommet to fit the waste pipe of a sink. He said, "Right, I want you to make a grommet for me."

So I made the grommet and gave it to him.

He said, "What the hell is this? What on earth do you think this is?"

I said, "Well, it's a grommet."

He said, "It's not what I showed you to do."

So I said, "If you want a better one, you make it."

He gave me such a clout that I went sideways, head over heels. I was a bit of a cheeky young beggar, but I didn't cheek him any more after that.

He had a hand on him like a sledgehammer.

One day Albert and I were sent down to a house in Mill End, to repair a ball valve in the loft. It was only a small job. I could have done it on my own, but I wasn't allowed to.

The house belonged to Mr Whitehead, my old headmaster. When he saw me, he said, "Oh, hello, Heckford. I see you are you doing something useful at last."

I said, "Yes, I am doing something now that even you can't do."

He turned his back and walked away – every dog has its day, doesn't it?

On another occasion, Albert Dowse and I were called to a house in Shire Lane in Chorleywood. The two old ladies who lived there had both been taken to hospital, so someone else was there to let us in.

We went into the loft to check the water in the storage tanks, and in the water were two dead starlings. They had contaminated the water, and these two ladies, instead of going downstairs to get fresh water, drank the water from the tap in the bathroom, which came from the storage tank in the loft. As a result, both the old ladies died.

From then on, we had the job of going round to all the big houses and making sure that they had covers on their storage tanks.

When it came to our lunch break, Dick Warner or Albert Dowse always tried to make sure we were close to The Gate, a public house on the Chorleywood–Rickmansworth Road. There we would have a hunk of bread with a hunk of cheese and a couple of nice large pickled onions. Although I was only fourteen, I used to have the same-size meal as the men, including a pint of beer to go with it.

On the pub sign outside The Gate there was a rhyme that said:

> This gate hangs well; it hinders none.
> Refresh and pay then carry on.

I learnt quite a lot in that plumbing job. All the pipes were made of lead in those days, and we had to solder the joints together. It was quite a skilled job, and I was able to do that kind of work by the time I was sixteen. I was trained in the plumbers' workshops in the yard. I became quite adept at that.

Then copper pipes began to replace the old lead ones, and I had to learn to join copper and lead pipes together to make one good pipe.

When I was sixteen, I took a day off and went over to Watford to volunteer for the navy, but they wouldn't have me, except as a boy seaman. I said I didn't want to go in as a boy seaman; I said I wanted to fight alongside the men.

They said, "Sorry, you are too young; we can't let you do that."

When I got home, my mother said, "Where have you been?" and, when I told her, she said, "You ungrateful little swine!"

She picked up the broom to give me a good wallop, but I caught the broom and said to her, "That's the last time you lay a hand on me" – which it was.

After that, I couldn't stay at home any more, so I phoned my aunt in Southend to see if I could go and live with her.

She said, "Denny, boy, I know the kind of life you have had; by all means come over as soon as you are ready."

That is how I came to leave Chorleywood and go to Hadleigh in Essex.

At Hadleigh I still had to carry on as an apprentice plumber. This time I was apprenticed to a man called Sid Keepance.

We had a terrible winter in 1946/7. It was a really wicked winter. Sid sent me out on jobs on my own, and – I am not kidding you – some of the jobs were vile. I had to remove full lavatory pans and knock out the frozen muck into the garden. Then I had to put in new pans.

I was doing a lot of this work completely on my own, but Sid was gaining all the money for it. I was working seven days a week for him, but I never got an extra penny in my pay packet.

One Monday, after a hard weekend, I decided I had had enough. I jumped on a bus and went straight to the recruitment centre in Romsford.

When I got there, the officer (a lieutenant) said, "Yes, what do you want?"

I said, "I have come to volunteer for the navy."

He said, "Well, have you filled in a form?"

I said, "No, I haven't filled in any forms, but I have come all the way from Hadleigh and I want to join the navy."

He said, "Well, you can't. They have just started the exams ten minutes ago. You are too late."

I said, "I am not leaving until I have joined."

Eventually the lieutenant gave in. He gave me the forms to fill in and he said, "Sit down over there at that table."

I did so, and within about ten minutes I'd completely finished all the examination papers.

He said to me, "Are you stuck?"

"No – I have finished," I replied.

He said, "Well, I am afraid you can't have passed in that time."

I said, "Well, you won't know until you have come and had a look, will you?"

He came and looked over my shoulder at the first page; then he looked at the second page; and then he looked at the third and the fourth pages, and so on.

He said, "Oh, my word! Yes, you are in."

And that was it.

He said, "How come you have done that so quickly? The others are still working away in there."

I said, "Well, I have not had to waste time trying to hide what I am doing from people who are trying to look over my shoulder and cheat; I was able to concentrate entirely on the questions, and I have done the whole thing off my own bat."

With that, he said, "Well, anyway, you are in. We will write and tell you when you are to go for your medical."

When I got back to work on Tuesday, Sid Keepance asked me where I had been, so I told him.

"You ungrateful little bugger!" he said. "I have gone to a lot of trouble to get you exempt because of your apprenticeship."

I said, "Well, I didn't ask you to get me exempt."

I was coming up to eighteen and a half, and until then I hadn't known he had got me exempt.

Sid tore up my apprenticeship papers and sacked me on the spot. In those days employees had far fewer rights than they do now.

As I walked down the road, I met the foreman of a new building site. I knew him fairly well and we often used to chat.

He said, "What on earth are you doing, coming back this way at this time of the day?" When I told him what had happened, he said, "Don't worry, lad – you can work with me on the building site until you go."

I ended up as a hod-carrier, and I became quite adept at running up ladders with a hod of bricks without even having to hold the hod.

When I went for my eye test, there was a young chap there who was colour-blind. Of course, he was told they couldn't accept him because he wouldn't be able to identify the signal flags. He cried with disappointment, which was a shame, but the officer said, "It's all right, old son. Don't worry – I have got a job for you in the marines."

Lord knows what job he had in mind for a colour-blind person.

Anyway, I passed my medical, and the next thing was that I received my papers directing me to go to HMS *St George*, a training school for naval ratings at Gosport.

CHAPTER 5: Naval Training

When I got to Waterloo Station, I was put in charge of a group of men. Some of them were Londoners, and they thought they were very clever, but I said to them, "You might think you are clever, but just remember this: I have been given authority to get you down to Gosport, and get you down there I will. If anybody disagrees with me, he answers to me."

We got down there quite safely. We got shipped over to Gosport, and then we went to HMS *St George*, where we were to do our training before being posted on to our ships.

The training wasn't always straightforward. We had a bit of a bully of a petty officer, but it was his job to bully us into shape. If we disobeyed an order, we ended up having to run around the parade ground, either with four-inch shells and casings on our shoulders, or with our rifles held above our heads. We daren't let them droop; we just had to keep going until he said enough was enough. Well, that was the kind of thing we didn't want too often

– believe me! We learnt very quickly to do what we had to do.

We had to learn everything to do with the rifle; marching; seamanship, which involved tying knots and splices and so forth; and we also had to do arithmetic.

After we had been there for about two months – or three months at the most – we were transferred to HMS *Anson*, a huge battleship. Life on HMS *Anson* was pretty straightforward; nothing untoward happened there. We used to go to sea to learn seamanship, and we had to go into classrooms to learn different splicings, and other basic things.

We were up at five o'clock in the morning, scrubbing the wooden decks in our bare feet. Boy, it used to be a bit cold – believe me! We hosed the decks with salt water and scrubbed them with big deck-scrubbers. We didn't mind it too much. We used to have a laugh between ourselves.

Afterwards we'd go down to have our showers. "Shit, shower, shave and shampoo," we called it, although we never shampooed.

Then we would go and have our breakfast before we went into the classrooms.

I don't know exactly how long I was on HMS *Anson,* but it seemed like for ever. It was probably no more than three months.

At last I was transferred to Royal Naval Barracks, Devonport, and from there I got my first seagoing ship, a destroyer called HMS *Dunkirk.* I applied to become an anti-aircraft gunner: others went for a different type of gunnery, signals, torpedo training and so forth.

We had quite an eventful time on HMS *Dunkirk*. Some of the time it was quite pleasant, and at other times it was unpleasant – which is natural. On the whole I had quite a good time.

We went for a cruise round the Mediterranean: Gibraltar, Malta and Tangiers. I was on the quarter-deck mess, which was way back aft. Getting meals there from the galley, especially in a bit of 'roughers' (rough seas) was a struggle. We had to go through a hatch and on to the mess.

In Tangiers, I bought some sugar to take home to Guz (our name for Devonport Dockyard), and I also bought a bottle of brandy.

When I went back on board, I stowed the sugar away ready for when I got home, and then we cracked open the brandy. A sailor called Birchy was asleep in his hammock, which was swung low between two stanchions, and someone reminded me that I had promised to save him a 'wet' (a drop of the brandy).

By that time I was a bit merry, so I tipped the bottle up and the poor chap nearly choked to death. I thought he was going to fill me in there and then. However, the other chaps calmed him down, and he took it all in good part in the end. I let him finish off the rest of the brandy by himself.

Apart from our training, we had to look after our

part of the ship, which, in my case, was the quarterdeck. The tour itself was quite uneventful, except that it was while I was on HMS *Dunkirk* that I qualified as an AA3 gunner.

When we returned, we docked at Londonderry, Ireland. About a dozen of us were told to manhandle a big hawser on board ship. It was very, very heavy, and I appeared to be the only one who was trying to lift it. I ended up by giving myself a hernia.

I was not allowed to do any more work, other than light duties. I still did my gunnery training, but I wasn't allowed to do any loading, or anything like that. I could only do the laying and the training of the automatic gear, and I could use the joystick.

The chief buffer used to give me a tin of tobacco and some cigarette papers and send me up into the nacelle, where the radar was. While the others were working, I would make cigarettes from his 'ticklers' (the old naval tobacco).

Eventually we sailed from Londonderry back to Plymouth, where they dumped me on the jetty with all my kit. They then sailed off again and left me stranded there.

After about twenty minutes or so, an ambulance came and took me to Stone House Hospital, where they repaired my hernia.

After the operation, I wouldn't let the surgeon come near my bed. There was a petty officer in the bed next to me, and he said I had been rather boisterous – especially language-wise. When the surgeon came round with the Sister, he said, "Ah, Sister, this is the chap with the wonderful vocabulary – am I right?"

She said, "Yes, sir, you are right."

The surgeon gave me a grin and said, "Well, you are doing well," and he cleared off.

We had to get up to have our meals, and one day – I am sure it was done on purpose – there was a six-inch worm on my plate. I flatly refused to eat the meal. When the Sister came round I pointed at the worm and said, "Well, if you fancy eating it, you do so – but I don't!"

She said, "Oh, get it down you – it's extra vitamins."

I still didn't touch it. I took it back to the galley, and I said to them, "If this is your idea of a joke, keep it!"

I just slung my dinner on the floor, and of course the plate smashed and the food went all over the place. I never got into trouble for it, but I suppose I shouldn't have reacted like that.

When I had my sick leave, I went to stay with a girl who lived in Sarrat. Her parents would let me stay for a few days and nights, but we had different rooms.

CHAPTER 6: HMS *Jamaica*

I heard that HMS *Jamaica* was sailing for the West Indies, so I immediately volunteered to be drafted on board. My request was granted, and I became a crew member of HMS *Jamaica*.

Before we sailed, we had Christmas leave. (It was all leave for me, wasn't it?) I spent some of it at my girlfriend's and some at my aunt's in Southend.

On board HMS *Jamaica*, my part of the ship was the fo'c's'le – that's at the sharp end.

For about ten days we were at Weymouth, and I got together with a girl I met there but I didn't keep in touch with her after that time. When we left harbour we had to muster on the fo'c's'le. We were called to attention and then stood at ease, and so forth and so on, and that was the beginning of our journey to the West Indies. It was a most enjoyable trip. On the way, we had to cross the equator, for which I became a member of King Neptune's court. I have got the certificate above my head now where I am sitting. The whole trip was quite a lot of fun. I didn't realise you could have quite as much fun in the navy.

When we arrived at Bermuda, our main port of call, I received a letter from my girlfriend to say she had met someone else; so it was the old heave-ho, but life went on as normal. We were in Bermuda for a few days to allow the skipper and other officers to make the acquaintance of the local bigwigs. We could go ashore, but our movements were limited. The only drink we could get was rum and coke – but that wasn't too bad really, was it?

Before we left the West Indies, we made a courtesy call at Jamaica, which our Colony-class ship was named after. We had a great time in Kingston. We were taken round the rum distillery, and we were all given samples. By the time we left the distillery, some of us were under the weather, so to speak. We managed to sample each different brew – and, believe me, there was some good stuff there, there really was!

After we had been in Kingston for about a week, we travelled round to Montego Bay – one of the most beautiful bays you could ever wish to go to. The sea was so clear you could see the anchor in the seabed. It really was something to see.

After a few days we sailed for Valparaíso in Chile, which meant we had to go through the Panama Canal. HMS *Jamaica* was the first British warship to go to the West Indies or to Valparaíso since before the war, and, believe me, they made a fuss of us.

The Panama Canal is absolutely wonderful.

H.M.S. JAMAICA — KOREAN VETERAN HOMEWARD BOUND

TWO DAYS IN MALTA

By a Staff Reporter

THE cruiser H.M.S. Jamaica (Captain J.S.C. Salter, D.S.O. and Bar, O.B.E.) entered Grand Harbour yesterday for a two-day stay on her voyage homewards from the Far East.

Jamaica was the first Royal Navy ship to enter the Korean waters in June 1950, the first to take part in a surface action with North Korean ships, the first United Nations warship to cross the 38th Parallel, the first ship to suffer casualties and the first ship to sight and sink mines.

She was also in action during September 13-19, 1950, in the first major landing of the Korean war at Inchon Straits being the first warship to open fire and shoot down a North Korean aircraft.

But as the ship slowly and almost unnoticed slipped into the Grand Harbour in the very early misty hours yesterday morning, she looked just like another warship come to anchor here.

Long Ago and Far Away

It all seems so very long ago to the 700 men aboard when "Jamaica" sailed from Plymouth on January 7, 1949, bound for the West Indies Station, to arrive at Bermuda 10 days later.

Korea was far, far away and unheard of then, while the pleasures of those "runs ashore" at Kingston, Jamaica, Valparaiso (via the Panama Canal), Coquimbo, Lima, Buenaventura, during a cruise to South America, were fresh in the minds of the crew.

"Jamaica" returned to the Royal Canadian Navy. Then on April 25 the Admiralty announced that "Jamaica" had been ordered to the Far East from Bermuda to take the place of the cruiser H.M.S. London which had been damaged when on April 21 she had

H.M.S. JAMAICA in Grand Harbour yesterday, with the Union Jack painted on the forward gun turret for air recognition purposes in the Korean war. The crew are at work cleaning and painting ship and (centre below, oil is being taken aboard from "Rowanol." The rating by the anchor, right, fell into the sea just after this photograph was taken. He suffered no ill effects.

tried to fight her way past the cruiser Communist guns in the Yangtse River to rescue wounded at Hong Kong via Pearl Harbour, on May 29, 1949, and Vice-Admiral A.C.G. Madden, C.B., C.B.E., Flag Officer Second in Command of the Far East Station hoisted his flag in the Pacific Ocean and arrived under fire.

"Cruising Down the River"

When the two ships met north of Formosa the Royal Marine Band from "Jamaica" played "Cruising down the river on a Sunday afternoon" as hundreds of Jollies lined the cruiser's rails, cheering and waving caps as "Americans" drew alongside.

"Jamaica" was active exercising during the last months of 1949 after a refit at Singapore. Further exercises to test the defences of Hong Kong were carried out early in 1950 and in February and March the cruiser combined with the U.S. Navy for exercises off the Philippines.

"Jamaica" sailed to Ominato, North of Japan in April as the advance party to set up a summer anchorage for the Fleet during the hot summer months. On return to Hong Kong the cruiser sailed with 42 Commando for Penang.

Start of Korean War

Then came the start of the summer cruise to Japan but the cruiser had hardly left Kure when the fighting in Korea flared up and she was ordered to sail to rendezvous with the Far East Fleet, later joining a U.S. Task Force off the east coast of Korea.

Jamaica was soon in action when with U.S.S. Juneau and H.M.S. Black Swan she took part on July 2, 1950, in the first surface action against enemy E-boats, claiming three of five boats sunk. That same day she was in action again in the first naval bombardment of the war — off Chumonjin.

Five days later "Jamaica" was the first ship to cross the 38th Parallel to bombard Yangyong causing much damage to the power station and other military objectives when 133 rounds were fired by her six-inch guns.

The following day, July 8, "Jamaica" suffered her first

casualties when six men were killed by a shell from a 75-mm shore battery bursting on the "Jamaica" while concentrated on patrol off the west coast of Korea from July to September, 1950. During September 13-19 the cruiser took part as a major unit of the bombarding force in the first big landing of the Korean war at Inchon.

More patrols off the west coast followed and on October 11 Captain Salter was decorated with the U.S. Bronze Star by Admiral Struble.

From June to October "Jamaica" steamed 23,676 miles and was at sea on and off for 74 days. Over 2,460 rounds were fired by the cruiser's six-inch guns during this period (as compared with 1,758 rounds fired in World War II) and over 1,074 rounds by the ship's four inch guns.

"Jamaica" was at Singapore to refit in October and is at present on her way home, having arrived here on Monday.

During World War II "Jamaica" (commissioned in May 1942) took part in Russian convoy actions, was at the North African landings at Oran, at the Battle of North Cape for the sinking of the German raider "Scharnhorst" and took part in other Atlantic operations. In June 1945 "Jamaica" conveyed Their Majesties the King and Queen to the Channel Islands.

Now the veteran of the Korean war is on her way home, having suffered casualties, and a certain amount of battering. She will soon be spick and span for all that. The morale of her crew has always been high, for "Jamaica" has been a very happy ship.

Night firing with the six-inch guns.

This was my gun after the action.

have been unable to continue ... s and radio will also make the
production. trip. ... directors ... representatives ...

THE 10,000-TON LIGHT CRUISER H.M.S. JAMAICA of the America and West Indies Squadron, which has been on a visit to Kingston, Port Antonio and Montego Bay since January 29, leaves today in continuation of her cruise.

HONG KONG, SUNDAY, MAY 29, 1949.   Price: 20 C

HMS Jamaica arrived here yesterday from Hamilton, Bermuda, to augment the Colony's naval strength, with Captain F. A. Ballance in command.

The 8,000-ton cruiser saluted the broad pennant of Commodore C. L. Robertson, R.N., of Hong Kong.

HMAS Bataan returned the salute.—("China Mail" photo)

LA...ND SEA CURFEW

To...

67

West Her
and Watford Re

THURSDAY, SEPTEMBER 21, 1

A. B. Dennis Pom-Poms
Dawn Attack

ADMIRAL PRAISES SHARPSHOOTING

Former Plumber Wins Five-Second Gun Duel

HERO in the quiet village of Chorleywood this week ——— former plumber who joined the Royal Navy three years ago, and on Sunday shot down the first enemy aircraft from a ship in the Korean war, ——— it made a dawn attack. He is 22-years-old Able-Seaman Dennis Heckford, of 26, Beechwood-cottages, The Swillett, Chorleywood.

When the news was sent from Korea on Sunday, the first person to tell Dennis's mother was a reporter. Mrs. Heckford was so alarmed that at first she thought something had happened to her son and she broke down.

Dennis is gunlayer of a pom-pom gun crew aboard the British cruiser "Jamaica," and with a five-second burst of fire brought down a Yak.

The crew were at ——— aircraft stations when a Stormovik dropped a bomb near an American cruiser two miles away from the "Jamaica," which formed part of the Korean invasion fleet. The Stormovik flew off when Dennis's crew, captained by a 28-years-old leading seaman ——— Gloucestershire, opened fire. ——— then a Yak dropped a bomb ——— the American ship.

DECK RAKED WITH CANNON SHELLS

The Yak, too, flew off, but one ——— believed to be a Yak ——— and raked the "Jamaica's" deck with cannon ——— machine-gun fire.

Dennis got the plane in his sights and could see his officers going way back at him. He kept firing and saw a ——— blob of smoke under the

plane's fuselage. It was that hit which brought the plane down, according to Dennis.

The Yak plunged into the water and brok ———

The victory was not without cost. A cannon shell exploded on the pom-pom gun mounting and severely wounded one rating.

Two others were less seriously injured. A machine gun bullet which hit the ship further aft wounded a fourth man.

PRAISE FROM REAR-ADMIRAL

The "Jamaica's" crew have been praised for their alertness and sharp shooting by American Rear-Admiral John M. Higgins, commanding the cruiser bombardment force.

Dennis, who is single, volunteered for seven years' service in the Royal Navy. Previously, he was a plumber for a firm of builders in Chorleywood.

A very quiet boy, Dennis used to spend most of his spare time before he joined the Navy in reading.

He is one of four brothers. One, Wilfred, is in the Army and the youngest, Brian, who is still at school, is a member of the A.T.C. in Rickmansworth.

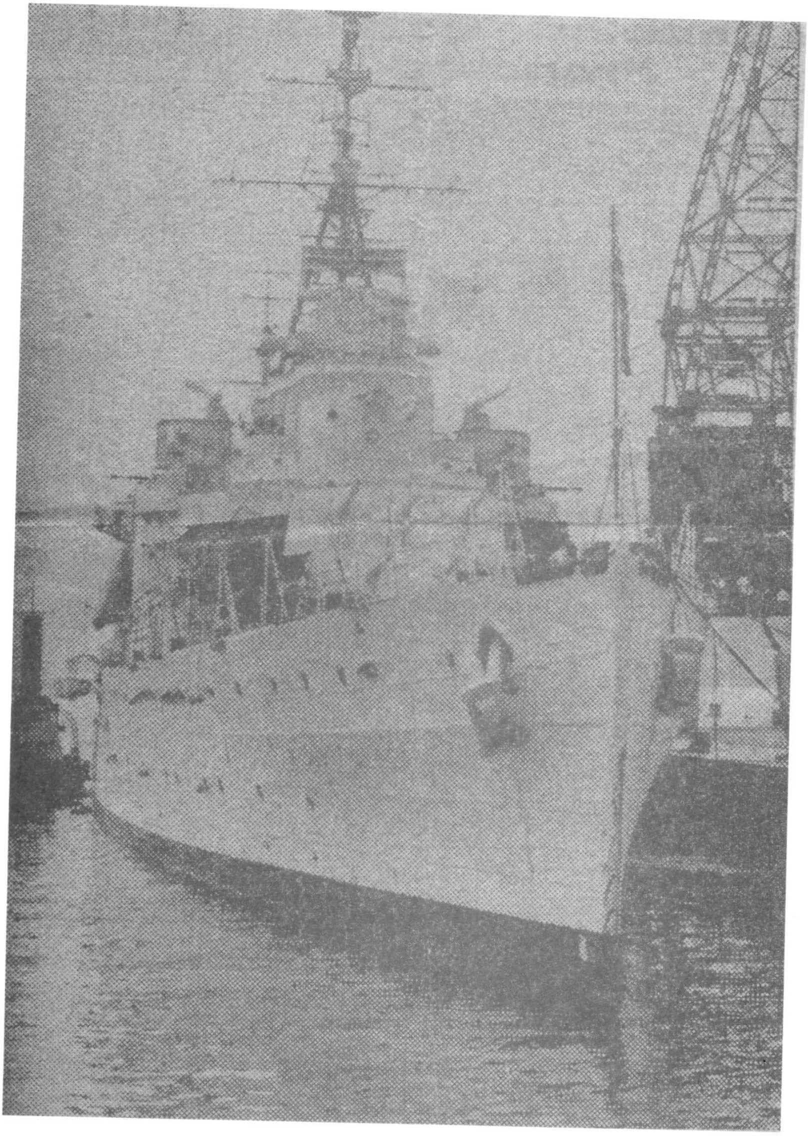

DENNIS'S POM-POM DOWNS A YAK

From FRANK GOLDSWORTHY: Off Inchon, Sunday

WITH a five-second burst of pom-pom fire from a British cruiser, Able-Seaman Dennis Heckford at dawn today shot down the first enemy aircraft to fall to the guns of any United Nations ship since the Korean war began.

ABLE-SEAMAN HECKFORD
A five-second burst . . .

Heckford, aged 22, single, of Beechwood Cottages, The Swille, Chorleywood, Hertfordshire, is gunlayer of the pom-pom crew captained by 28-year-old Leading-Seaman George Ralph, of Friday-street in the Gloucestershire village of Arlingham.

The West Country crew of this ship, at repel aircraft stations, saw a Stormovik sweep down and drop a bomb near an American cruiser two miles away on the fringe of the great United Nations invasion fleet.

We opened fire and the aircraft turned away. It was followed immediately by a Yak, which also dropped a bomb near the American cruiser.

SAW TRACERS

Then one of the planes, believed to be the Stormovik, turned towards us. As it approached it raked the deck with cannon and machine-gun fire.

Said Heckford later: "As I got him in my sights I could see my tracers going one way and his coming straight back towards me. As I kept firing I saw a little black blob of smoke under his fuselage and I think that hit brought him down."

The plane banked steeply, passed about 30 feet above our fo'c'sle, plunged into the water 50 yards away, and broke up as it bounced over the waves. A wheel has been recovered.

A cannon shell exploded on Heckford's pom-pom gun mounting. It severely wounded one rating—who was transferred to a hospital ship—and slightly wounded two others. A fourth rating had a flesh wound from an armour-piercing machine-gun bullet hitting the ship nearly 100 yards further aft.

ADMIRAL PRAISES

A midshipman escaped when bullets smashed two dials of the predictor he was working.

A Stormovik and a Yak, making a dawn attack with one bomb each, damaged the destroyer Comus in this area several weeks ago.

These are the only enemy air attacks on shipping reported since early July.

American Rear-Admiral John M. Higgins, commanding the cruiser bombardment force, signalled: "Your alertness and sharp shooting deserve the highest praise. Deeply regret injuries to your gallant men."

Vice-Admiral Arthur Struble, commanding the 7th Fleet, signalled: "Well done."

Yesterday I went into Inchon with Admiral Struble. He was seeking means of speeding up further

BRITISH NAVY PUSSER'S RUM - THE TOT IS BACK

Today you have the opportunity to taste the superb rum which for more than 300 years was an essential part of daily life aboard the ships of the Royal Navy. First introduced in 1655 in the West Indies Station as an alternative to beer, which did not keep, by 1731 Pusser's Rum was in general use. Onboard ship the stores are controlled by the Purser and over the centuries the sailors corrupted this to 'Pusser', thus everything originating from Naval stores was 'Pusser's' and this is still the case today.

In 1731 the ration was ½ pint of Pusser's Rum per man per day, helping to make the rigours of shipboard life more bearable. However, in 1740, Admiral Vernon, concerned with quarrelling and drunkeness in the Royal Navy, issued an order that the rum should be mixed with water to alleviate the problem. This gave great offence to the sailors who had previously nicknamed Admiral Vernon 'Old Grog', from the grogram cloak he wore. Thus they called the watered rum after him as well. Therefore, true 'grog' is Pusser's Rum and water. Admiral Vernon further decreed that the rum and water should be mixed in a barrel adapted for the purpose. Thus originated the oak rum tub with the familiar 'The Queen God Bless Her' in brass lettering.

As conditions onboard ship improved over the years and modern ships became increasingly technical, so the rum ration was reduced, until it was finally discontinued on 31st July, 1970. On that day the Admiralty issued the following signal from the First Sea Lord:-

>   'Personal'   From First Sea Lord.
>
>   "Most farewell messages try, to jerk a tear from the eye,
>   But I say to you lot, very sad about tot,
>   But thank you, good luck and good-bye".

Thus, after more than 300 years, Pusser's Rum was no more and the Admiralty donated the money which would have been used to purchase one year's supply to the Royal Navy Sailors' Fund, 'The Tot Fund', which is used to provide amenities for serving personnel. Today, Pusser's Rum is again available for sale to the general public with Admiralty permission to use the name, the original blend and the White Ensign. In return, a substantial donation from the sale of each bottle of Pusser's Rum is made to 'The Tot Fund'.

Pusser's Rum today is blended from the same five rums from Demerara and Trinidad that were used by the Royal Navy for the daily 'Up Spirits' issue and is marketed in the United Kingdom by E. D. & F. Man Limited, the exclusive Admiralty Rum Brokers from 1797 until 1970.

For further details and availability information, please contact Michael Fogg or Michael Thomason, E. D. & F. Man Limited, Sugar Quay, Lower Thames Street, London, EC3R 6DU. Telephone (01) 626 8788.

The History: British Navy Pusser's Rum™

The sailor's mess between the guns

For well over 300 years, from before the days of Nelson, wooden ships and iron men, the Royal Navy dispensed its Pusser's Rum. First introduced into the Navy in 1655 on the West Indies Station as an alternative to beer which did not keep, by 1731 it was in general use. The ration was then two gills (½ pint) of neat rum a day divided into two issues: one in the forenoon and one in the afternoon.

The navy of rum in the Navy, is largely that of social change, both in England and the Royal Navy. From 1850 and throughout the 18th century, shipboard life was incredibly difficult, and to make life bearable rum played its part in reducing sensitivity. And often, in those days, battles were fought eye-ball-to-eyeball, so to speak. Personnel requirements were different in the old Navy; the mental alertness for packing a cannonball into a muzzle loader was far different than that required to operate a modern weapons system.

The rum issue was finally abolished in 1970. The reasons for abolition were much the same as for reductions in the past, that is the men were much more efficient without it, and in a highly technical and sophisticated Navy no risk or margin for error which might be attributable to rum could be allowed.

So it was that on August 1st, 1970, tradition ended. The last tot of Pusser's Rum was drunk aboard Their Majesties' Ships. Round the world glasses were raised in their final salute. "The Queen's" they said, and it's no exaggeration to say that at that moment many a strong man had a tear in his eye, at the passing of a tradition so old and fine — thus rum was no more.

British Navy Pusser's Rum revives the memories of that tradition — and is the same superb rum that was standard issue aboard ships of the Royal navy at the time of the rum issue's termination in 1970. When the rum was discontinued, the Admiralty donated to a new fund the amount of money which would have been used to purchase a one year's supply of Pusser's Rum. This fund provides recreational equipment and facilities outside of Admiralty's budget. This endowment, the Royal Navy Sailors' Fund — but more commonly called "The Tot Fund" — receives a substantial donation from the sale of each bottle of British Navy Pusser's Rum. Thus the association of Pusser's Rum and the Navy still carries forward as it has for 350 years, and the British Navy Pusser's Rum tradition still lives!

British Navy Pusser's Rum

A blend of the same 5 rums from Demerara and Trinidad that were used by the Royal Navy in the production of their celebrated "Pusser's Rum" for who it was the Navy was famous. Just now, than 300 years British tars drank their Pusser's Rum and for many of the men its daily issue with the sacrosanct ritual which accompanied it, it was the highlight of their day. British Navy Pusser's Rum is the same superb rum that was, constantly termination, August 1st, 1970. Pusser's Rum tastes no different and unsurpassed by any other. It may be best appreciated by sipping it on the rocks or a t. Long with or without a touch of lime. Its dark color is also in keeping with tradition, for the rum was always darkened to camouflage any cloudiness which might have been present in the water when it was mixed with the rum to produce the traditional Grog. Pusser's Rum is 95.5 proof as was the regulation issue in the British Navy

The Name 'Pusser's'

A corruption of the word "purser", for hundreds of years Royal Navy sailors have referred to the "purser" as "pusser" — and anything which came from the purser was called "pusser's" — and still is today!

Grog

Traditional Grog is two parts water and one part Pusser's Rum. The name was coined by British tars about the middle of the 18th century. Until this time their

Photo credit: Commanding Officer HMS Victory

Pusser's Rum always been served 'neat', that is without water. Admiral Vernon, a highly esteemed officer, changed all this. He ordered that the rum be mixed with water to reduce drunkenness. This gave great offense to the tars, and since they'd nicknamed him 'Old Grog' from the program boat-cloak he wore on the quarterdeck when the weather was up, they called the watered rum 'Grog' after him as well. So true 'Grog' is Pusser's Rum and water

Rum Tub

'Grog' was issued from the Rum Tub to 1 ½ rating rates and ½ below, each man being issued one tot daily. Chief Petty Officers and Petty Officers received their tot neat (without water) - direct from the Spirit Room. The distribution of neat rum - or 'Sneakers' - as it was called - took place at 1100 hours daily when the bos'n piped 'Up Spirits' to herald the event. The issue of Grog followed one hour later.

Copper Measures

The copper measures were used for the collection and measuring of rum and Grog. A set consisted of the seven shown ranging in size from the one gallon to the ¼ gill - commonly called the 'tot' because it was the ½ gill that carried eventually as the standard daily issue. So a 'tot' of rum is ½ gill or ⅛th of a pint. Officers were not entitled an issue of rum except on special occasions.

Alpha-Delta-28

This is the signal flown by ships of the British Navy when they 'Splice the Main Brace' which in the past indicated that a double issue of rum was forthcoming for a special occasion or a job well done; special occasions being such events as a royal birthday or a Royal wedding. In the present day the signal is also flown to welcome guests aboard for free drinks. Note that the '2' and the '8' are different from the International Code Flags used by the merchant marine and yachtsmen.

Royal Navy Rum Terminology

Grog: Traditionally, 2 parts water, 1 part Pusser's Rum. *Tot:* ⅛th pint rum, the standard daily ration. *Neat:* Rum without water. *Sippers:* A small gentlemanly sip from a friend's rum issue. *Gulpers:* One, but only one, big swallow from another's tot. *Sandy Bottoms:* To see off whatever's in a mug when offered by a friend. *Splice the Main Brace:* A double tot for a job well done, or an invitation aboard for free drinks. *The Framework of Hospitality:* Where 3 sippers equal 1 gulp, and 3 gulps equal 1 tot!

Pusser's Ltd., Road Town, Tortola, British Virgin Islands. (809) 494-3467

At Pearl Harbour en route to Hong Kong sailing from Bermuda and the West Indies.

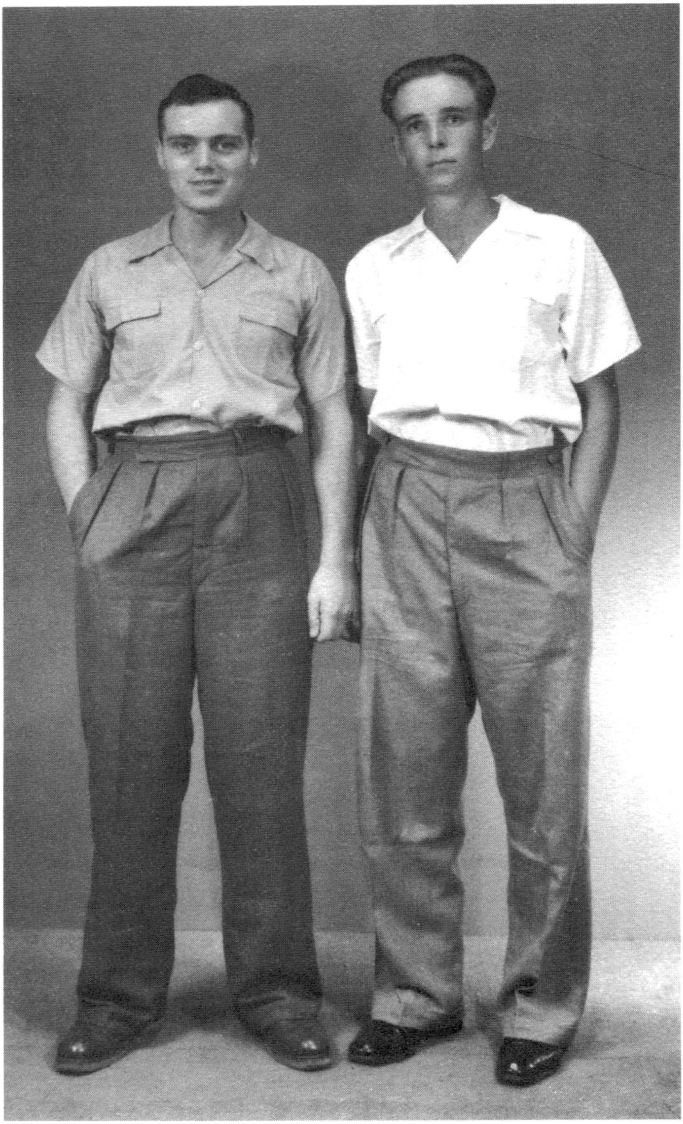

Symo and myself.

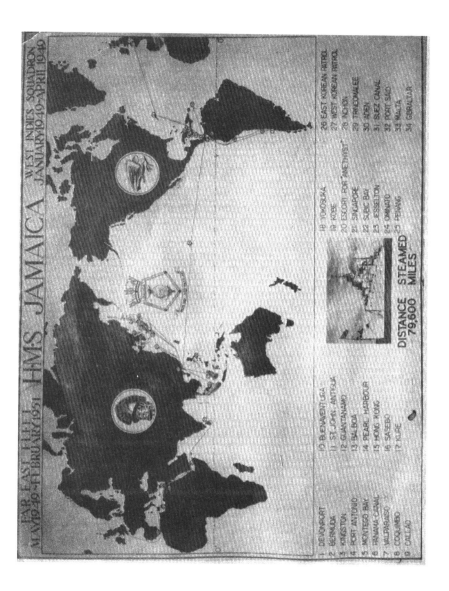

FAR EAST FLEET HMS **JAMAICA** WEST INDIES SQUADRON
MAY 1949~FEBRUARY 1951 JANUARY 1940~APRIL 1940

1. DEVONPORT
2. BERMUDA
3. KINGSTON
4. PORT ANTONIO
5. MONTEGO BAY
6. PANAMA CANAL
7. VALPARAISO
8. COQUIMBO
9. CALLAO

10. BUENAVENTURA
11. ST JOHN, ANTIGUA
12. GUANTANAMO
13. BALBOA
14. PEARL HARBOUR
15. HONG KONG
16. SASEBO
17. KURE

18. YOKOSUKA
19. KOBE
20. ESCORT FOR AMETHYST
21. SINGAPORE
22. SUBIC BAY
23. ESSELTON
24. OMINATO
25. PENANG

26. EAST KOREAN PATROL
27. WEST KOREAN PATROL
28. INCHON
29. TRINCOMALEE
30. ADEN
31. SUEZ CANAL
32. PORT SAID
33. MALTA
34. GIBRALTAR

DISTANCE STEAMED
79,600 MILES

75

WARRIOR

HAUL TOGETHER

This is to Certify that

D. S. Heckford. A/B

commissioned H.M.S. Warrior

1953-1954.

Captain,
Royal Navy.

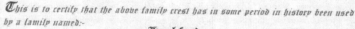

This is to certify that the above family crest has in some period in history been used by a family named:-

Heckford

or an etymological variant of that name.

Historic reference sources show the crest to be,

Upon an esquire's helmet a wreath, thereon, a pomegranate.

Heraldry can be defined as a system of symbolism. Originally crests were self assumed and generally depicted the characteristics of the bearer.

The pomegranate is the symbol of fertility and abundance.

In the middle ages something had to be done to enable the ordinary soldier to recognise his leader. So, the crests original purpose was to identify commanders in the heat and confusion of battle.

The flowing material which falls from the helmet is called the mantling. It not only served as protection against the elements, but also helped to tangle the thrusts of an opponent's sword in battle. Thus, it often became hacked and tattered, this is depicted on the modern mantling as proof of courage in battle. The helmet not only served as protection for the wearer, but also denoted rank, dependent upon the type and position of the helmet.

Origin and Meaning of

HECKFORD

HECKFORD is a locational surname of Anglo - Saxon origins. The employment in the use of the second name as a hereditary surname evolved around patronymics (first name of the father taken as the surname of the son), nicknames, locational, and occupational sources. The parish records of the Heckfords in co. Essex record the name interchangeabley with Hickford. It is locational to Hickford, a spot in co. Salop. Sir Robert Atkyns in his Ancient and Present State of Gloucestershire, says that "The Hickfords were an ancient family in co. Salop", originally styled Hugford. About the reign of James 1 the surname was turned into Higford, Hickford and Heckford. The latter also gave name to Heckford Park in co. Dorset. The derivation of the name is of the Old English Hyge which means "Mind, Mood, Courage" and Forde, "A Ford". Hyge was a personal name amongst the Anglo - Saxons. The name refers to the ancient tribal settlement of "The Ford of the Hyge Family". The name evolved as a hereditary surname during the Middle English period (circa 13th century).

EARLIEST REGISTRATIONS:
Edith Hicford co. Oxford, 1273 Ref: ROTULI HUNDREDORUM.
Baptised - Edward Heckford, Father-Edward Heckford, 1-2-1573 Ref: COLD NORTON, ESSEX.
Baptised - Abell Heckford, Father-Abell Heckford, FRATING, ESSEX.
Married - Daniel Hickford and Sarah, 20-7-1646 Ref: GREAT WIGBOROUGH, ESSEX.

COATS OF ARMS were used by the ancient world warlike nations on their shields and standards as distinguishing devices. The origins of badges and emblems may be traced to the earliest times and the art of blazoning these colours and emblems is called Heraldry, a name derived from the Old High German Heer, a host, an army, and Held, a champion. Heralds of old blazoned arms by Tinctures, Precious Stones and Planets.

COLOURS	TINCTURES	PRECIOUS STONES	PLANET
Yellow	Or	Topaz	Sol
White	Argent	Pearl	Luna
Black	Sable	Diamond	Saturn
Red	Gules	Ruby	Mars
Blue	Azure	Sapphire	Jupiter
Green	Vert	Emerald	Venus
Purple	Purpure	Amethyst	Marcu

THE ANCIENT ARMS OF THE HECKFORD FAMILY ARE RECORDED UNDER HICKFORD:
Arms - AZURE ON A FESS BETWEEN THREE LEOPARDS FACES ARGENT, THREE PELLETS.
Arms recorded in Burkets General Armory.

Sometimes, as we were going through, we could barely see the shoreline on either side; at other times we passed through very narrow gorges. It was a red-hot, wonderful experience.

We had never seen a welcome like the one we had in Chile. They put on a huge party for us, and everything was absolutely great.

One day, I was part of the duty watch when the boat returned from shore leave. One of our crew was lying in the bottom of the boat, and it looked as though he had been knifed or something. It looked as though there was blood all over him. However, what had happened was that he had become intoxicated with red wine, and then he had brought it up again all over his front. They had to manhandle him back on board because he was unable to stand.

When my two mates and I went into the city, a traffic policeman called us across to him. He pulled out a flask and made us have a drink with him while the traffic was building up all round. He didn't give a darn about the traffic; he was just interested in giving us this drink. Eventually we carried on our way, and the traffic was able to flow again.

We were in Valparaíso for quite a few days, and I got to know a gentleman called Mr Ashlin. He had lost his own son (I don't know how, because I didn't ask), and he took a liking to me because I resembled his son. He used to take us to restaurants to have a meal with him. Mr Ashlin said that when

I had finished with the navy I could go over to Chile and he would teach me everything he knew about civil engineering.

We also met a lovely Norwegian family, who welcomed us with open arms and gave us a meal and wine. Wherever we went in Valparaíso that is how we were treated. It was absolutely fantastic.

In South America, when we were in port, we had a visitors' day, where local people were invited on board ship. Some of the lads used to smuggle girls (usually prostitutes) down to the mess decks, but that was brought to a halt. They put guards of the duty watch at each hatchway so that nobody could even think of taking a girl down there.

While we were in Valparaíso, Nobby Clark and I were ordered into the dinghy, to go round and patch up the Plimsoll line with black paint.

When we were between the jetty and the ship, old Nobby Clark looked down and said, "Hey, Hank, look down!" Below us was a bloody great big ray. It was bigger than the dinghy.

We shot back round to the ship's ladder, and the officer of the watch wanted to know why the hell we were coming back on board.

He wouldn't believe us at first, but the ray was still there, and when he saw it he said, "Oh, my God! It is a whopper. Come back on board."

We had heard that a ray could easily sink a dinghy, so we never did finish painting the Plimsoll line.

We then moved to Coquimbo where the train ran straight down the main road of the town. It was quite something.

At Coquimbo we saw a young lady lift up her skirt and piddle like a man, and the young chap she was with was doing the same, up against the train wheels. We had never seen anything like it before. We were green matelots, let's face it! However, some of the older hands said they had seen it all before.

The people of Coquimbo gave us a big ranch party – and, believe me, that was some party! Two hundred and fifty of us attended. A fully grown steer was roasted on a spit over a great big open fire. There were also twenty barrels of beer. We called it onion beer because the following day everybody smelt of onions. It was rather a strange effect.

The rancher owned some racehorses, and he allowed some of us to ride some of his most expensive horses. The one I got was quite a big chestnut stallion. It was a lovely horse. All we had was a blanket and a bridle; there was no saddle or stirrups. We had to grip the horse with our legs. We galloped across a field towards a gate on the other side, but my horse decided it wanted to go towards the fence, which was about seven foot high. I thought, 'Oh, Christ, no! Any minute now he is going to try to jump that fence.' I pulled back on the reins and I managed to stop him short of the fence, but – I am not kidding! – I nearly shit myself.

I managed to canter back to the ranch, and when I told them about it the ranch people said, "Well, he is a jumper; he does go over the sticks." Apparently, the week before he had won quite a big race.

By then the meal was ready for us. We had great chunks of beef, loads of vegetables and, of course, lots of beer.

It wasn't bad beer. It was quite strong as well, and quite a few of the lads got a bit drunk on it. Those of us who were still sober had to get them back on board in one piece at the end of the evening.

The party they gave us was absolutely out of this world, and I will never ever forget the generous way they treated us. They were marvellous people.

The Mayor of Coquimbo gave a big dance and reception in a huge hall. I was on duty with five other ratings and an officer, and our job was to make sure nobody from our ship got into any mischief. Every now and again some of the ladies who had been at the big feast at the ranch recognised us, and they kept giving us drinks. By the time the evening ended, when we had to clear everybody out of the dance hall and make sure they got back on board, we were three parts cut as well. We had a job to march in decent order, and our petty officer wasn't too good either. However, we managed to get back on board, and we stood to attention while he reported us back on board. We really did have to work hard to appear sober.

From Coquimbo we went up to Lima, in Peru. When we got there, we had a lovely party at the Lima Cricket Club. Afterwards, they took us back to the dockyard, and we didn't have to pay taxi fares or anything.

A certain lieutenant, my divisional officer (I won't mention his name, because if he is still alive he would be embarrassed) did come back to the ship in a taxi, and he shouted to me to give him some money to pay the fare. I just stuck two fingers up at him and walked on. When I got back on board, I reported to the officer of the watch that there was an officer making a spectacle of himself, so the duty petty officer and two guards with their gaiters on went along, paid the taxi and brought him back on board. He didn't get into trouble or anything, but at one time he had been quite an unsociable person to me for some reason so at last I had got a little bit of my own back, hadn't I? I noticed afterwards that he still had it in for me a bit, but I just rode along with it.

In Lima, no one was allowed to go down a certain street because of the brothels. All the buildings had half doors, like stable doors, and the prostitutes leant over the doors, more or less showing their wares – no bras or anything like that.

One day we were passing one of these buildings where three prostitutes were standing and looking out. When they called out to us, Ted Hammet – he was a bit of a boy – shook a bottle of lemonade and squirted it all over them. The police came, gathered us all together and marched us down to the other end of the street before they would release us. The prostitutes were protected by law, and what we did was a misdemeanour, so we were lucky to get away with it, weren't we?

From Peru we went up to a place called Buenaventura. We anchored in a huge bay, where there were no other ships at all. We weren't allowed ashore at first because there was a civil war going on between the army and the police. The army were in the forest and the police were in the town. There was quite a bit of gunfire.

Later they held an armistice and each watch was allowed ashore for a short time. We were not allowed to go outside the perimeter of the town, and we were informed that if we went towards the jungle, we could be shot. Naturally, we adhered to the rules and stayed in the town, but there was nothing there worth seeing. I don't understand why we were called there, unless it was for diplomatic reasons.

There were hundreds of pelicans in the harbour, and many of us had never seen them before. They were quite amusing, but we soon lost interest in them.

After a couple of days we sailed for Antigua and had a short spell there. Then we went back through the Panama Canal and called at Jamaica and then

Bermuda, where we went into dry dock, to have the ship's bottom scraped and cleaned.

While we were in Bermuda our ship's football team won the West Indies Shield, or West Indies Cup – something like that. When we came out of dry dock, HMS *Sheffield* took our place.

At this time the *Amethyst* was caught up the Yangtze River, so we had to return the cup or shield (whichever it was) and then set sail for Hong Kong. If HMS *Sheffield* hadn't been in dry dock, she would have gone instead. Anyway, we were fortunate enough to go through the Panama Canal for the third time. Most matelots are lucky if they ever go through the Panama Canal once, but we were able to boast of going through three times on a naval warship. Small traction engines, called 'donkeys', towed the ships through the locks of the canal.

CHAPTER 7: The Far East

On the way to Hong Kong, we stopped at Pearl Harbor. We were only there for twelve hours just to refuel, but each watch had six hours ashore. The port watch had six hours and then the starboard watch had six hours.

We did have some entertainment from the hula-hula girls, but not much, and we had to stay in a certain area, where the PX stores was.

When the twelve hours was up, we set sail again and arrived safely in Hong Kong. It took twenty-eight days altogether, with just that one stop, but we didn't get bored; we had plenty to do and we could make plenty of our own amusements.

After being in Hong Kong for a week or so, we then went for a cruise which included Singapore and Borneo.

In Borneo, we were allowed to go swimming in a bay where there were one or two small hammerhead sharks, but they didn't interfere with us. We also had to watch out for jellyfish. I was one of the few that swam; the others rowed to the shore, bringing their equipment, including rifles. What the hell we had rifles for I don't know. We didn't need them.

Two of the blokes (Smithy and Gavin were their names) went into the jungle and annoyed a group of apes by throwing stones at them. The whole bloody group of apes came out of the jungle, and they chased us off the beach. We had to get back into the boat and row out to safety, because they were throwing everything they could at us. That ended our little trip round to that bay.

When I look back now, it seems quite funny, but at the time we weren't amused. We had a right old go at old Smithy and Gavin.

A couple of days later, we were invited to go into the jungle with the Dayak headhunters. All very interesting it was. They told us to keep our eyes open for wild boar, but before we had time to unsling our rifles from our shoulders a big boar came tearing towards us. A petty officer stood directly in line with it, but he didn't have chance to fire his gun. The Dayak stepped forward and, with one slash of his big knife, he ripped open the boar's throat and killed it.

He said, "Well, that will make a good feast."

After that little escapade, the most interesting wild animals we saw were the monkeys.

When we arrived back in Hong Kong, I was amongst the crew selected to man a motor fishing vessel (MFV). It didn't have any guns, apart from my Bren gun. Our officer, Lieutenant Commander Brooker, used to bring beer on board, so we could have a beer at midday and when we got back at night to the ship in Hong Kong. Then we would get our tot and have a decent dinner, which we didn't get on board the MFV. This was our routine for about ten days.

When we were in Mirs Bay, most of our time we were swimming, but we also had to keep our eyes open for pirates. If anything came towards us, we got out of the water, back into our MFV, and I had to run below deck to get my Bren gun, which I wasn't allowed to keep on deck. The junks would sidle up fairly close, and we never knew which of them were pirate vessels until they opened fire. They would have an old-fashioned cannon mounted on the big poop deck, and they filled it with nails and nuts and bolts and screws – you name it, it was in there. And of course they fired. They never hit us at any time, but by the time I had fetched my Bren gun they would be disappearing from sight. I never had a chance to fire a shot at them, so it was a waste of time, basically, wasn't it?

Nevertheless, we had a lot of fun in those days. Our leading seaman was called Brooks, so we had Brooks and Brooker. Lieutenant Commander Brooker was a gentleman officer, he really was, and Leading Seaman Brooks (Brooksie) was very, very easy-going as long as we didn't take advantage, so we had quite a relaxing time on that boat.

We eventually left Hong Kong when HMS *Jamaica* was assigned to take 42nd Commando to Malaya.

Some of the commandos were billeted on our mess deck, and I was given the job of catering for them, which included issuing their tot of rum. (They had a tot of rum, the same as we did, every day whilst they were on board.) I got to know some of them very, very well.

Eventually we arrived up at Kuala Kangsar, and they went inland to their base at Kuala Panang.

We stayed there for a few days before we sailed back to Hong Kong again.

The *Amethyst* was about to make her run, so we had to get down to the mouth of the Yangtze River and await her arrival. When she finally reached us, after running the gauntlet of the guns on the way down, we were there to protect her. She sailed out around us, and we took her to HMS *Consort* that was waiting to escort her back to Hong Kong.

The *Amethyst* was not a pretty sight, because she was holed from the shells – poor old girl! She had been through it, that girl. As she was escorted back to Hong Kong, we protected her flank on the seaward side.

At Hong Kong, her crew were taken off and billeted in some nice, clean, safe quarters. Some of HMS *Jamaica*'s ship's company had to go on board to clean up *Amethyst*'s inboard (below deck, including all the mess sections).

I wasn't one of the cleaners, but I did go on board just for a small visit. I shouldn't have done, but I did because one of my mates was in the cleaning crew. Some of the crew had kept rats as pets.

The squalor on the mess deck was appalling. They had been up the Yangtze River for a hell of a long time without proper facilities, and they just had to keep themselves clean as best they could. Some friends I met up with were on the *Black Swan*, which also used to take stores up the Yangtze River, and they told me the *Amethyst* had plenty of stores on board so they didn't run short of food.

Just after that, we set sail on another cruise, which included Singapore again. Singapore was our other depot, and that was where the dry dock was.

Whilst we were there, in dry dock, I put my name down as a volunteer to join the 42nd Commando Royal Marines for a while. I think there were about ten of us, including a petty officer. The 42nd Commando were patrolling the jungle in search of bandits.

Our guides (Dayak and Iban headhunters from Borneo) were absolutely marvellous. They could tell how long it was since bandits had been through.

The trail led up and up through mountainous country and it rained non-stop. Every two hours we had to burn the leeches off our bodies with cigarettes. We couldn't pull them off, or the wound would turn septic. I have never known anything like it.

Eventually the officer in charge said, "We are not going any further."

The Dayaks didn't want to turn back and they got very cross. They still wanted to go after the bandits and get their scalps. Apparently the scalps used to include both ears, which they cut off with their knives. I suppose that's why they were called headhunters.

Anyway, we turned back and eventually we made our way back down the mountainside, we were in single file, and we were sliding down on our backsides a hell of a lot of the time. I brought up the rear because I had got the Bren gun.

Suddenly there was a hell of a crack and a bullet whizzed past my head. We all dropped down because we thought we had been ambushed, and the marine officer came belting back up. He was shouting, "Everybody all right? Everybody all right?"

He got to me and I said, "Yes, I am fine, but it was a hell of a close one."

"Where did it come from?" he said.

I said, "Well, it came from ahead."

Suddenly the chap in front, a sailor who was the wireless operator, stood up with his rifle between his fingers and said, "I'm sorry – it was me." He had been carrying his rifle over his shoulder with the barrel facing upwards, and his safety catch had got knocked off while we had been sliding down. He was playing with the trigger, and of course the bloody thing went off, didn't it? I reckon the bullet missed my head by about an inch. I was that close to being a severe casualty, if you want to put it that way, but I could laugh about it afterwards.

From then on, as well as carrying the Bren gun and its tripod, I had to carry that bloke's rifle. So I was well laden until we got back to camp.

Somebody was looking after me while we were in that jungle!

One night some of our mates in the marine commandos took us to a village, where we visited a brothel. We weren't allowed in there, but we went. Suddenly someone shouted that the redcaps were coming, and we had to dive through a big trap door. We stayed doggo underneath the brothel until the redcaps cleared off, then we all crawled out and made our way back to the barracks. Oh boy, that was a do, that was!

Later we went to a huge dam for a day out, with a load of rations and stuff, and we lazed about and enjoyed ourselves. It was a very nice place.

Although by this time the refit was finished and HMS *Jamaica* was out of dry dock, we were still allowed ashore.

On one occasion Johnny Michaels, Simo and Ted Hammet went for a few beers and suchlike, and we had so little money that when we got back to HMS *Terror* (our barracks in Singapore) we had to beg the officer of the watch for money to pay the taxi driver.

When the tide was out, bandits could come across to Singapore, and sometimes they got into the sports ground of HMS *Terror*. Therefore the sports ground was out of bounds.

There was a swimming pool in the middle of the sports ground, and one night, after a few bevvies, I said, "Come on – let's go for a swim."

Although I was in my best whites, I dived in – well, flopped in, perhaps I should say.

I came up in the middle of the pool to hear Simo and Ted shouting, "Don't shoot! Don't shoot! Don't shoot! That's Heckford."

Around the pool were a load of matelots with their rifles all pointing at me, but luckily Simo and Ted managed to stop them from shooting.

I got marched back up to the barracks again, and they gave me a good dressing-down. I must have looked a pitiful sight, because I was wringing wet in my best white suit. I was marched back into our mess block, where I had a shower and changed into some dry clothes.

We always had to wash and iron our own clothes, which on this occasion wasn't too hard a job. However, I am reminded of a time during our cruise when I ended up covered in battleship-grey paint.

I was talking to the cleaners on F1 pom-pom, on the starboard side of the gun deck, when somebody dabbed a paintbrush in my back. I turned round, and Jock Cameron was standing there with the paintbrush in his hand. Jock was a short, strongly built fellow. I also had a paintbrush in my hand, so I dabbed him back. Then we stood there face-to-face, just striking each other with our paintbrushes. Soon we were literally covered in battleship-grey paint.

Petty Officer Hurley came up and gave us a bit of a bollocking and took us up to the skipper on the bridge.

On the way up, I said to Jock Cameron, "Oh well, we had a bit of fun there, didn't we, Jock? And the other blokes enjoyed it, didn't they?"

When we got in front of the skipper, we were so covered in paint that all he could see was our eyes. He turned away to have a good laugh, and then he turned back again. Petty Officer Hurley said he had brought us up because we were scrapping with paintbrushes instead of getting on with our work, and he reported my remark that we had had a bit of fun.

The skipper was very good; he just said, "Well, as you have been mucking about in my time, you can do a couple of extra hours of duty work on board this ship tonight."

Well, it couldn't be anywhere else, because we were at sea!

From Singapore we went back to Hong Kong, and after being in Hong Kong for another short spell we then put to sea again for another cruise, which included Japan.

Our first port of call was Tokyo, where we went ashore.

We also visited Nagasaki, where we saw a scene of sheer devastation. There was no building standing or anything.

After that we went to Kobi. We weren't allowed to go very far inland because it was a bit dodgy there. We were restricted in where we could go. However, one day we were invited to put our names down if we were interested in climbing a nearby mountain, and the following day we were on our way up it. We got more or less to the top in all the snow, and we came down most of the way on our backsides. We didn't have rifles this time, so there was no chance of another bullet whistling past me. We did have a lot of fun on that trip.

From there we went round to Kuri, and whilst we were in Kuri I met up with a nice young American girl. She was called by her initials BG. (Barbara Geathard was her name.) I used to visit her in her parents' home. Jimmy the One, our first lieutenant, also visited.

CHAPTER 8: The Korean War

After about a week, we had to carry on with the cruise. Well, we had only been gone from Kuri about two hours when we had to return there a bit sharp to refuel because the Korean War had started.

We went alongside a tanker to refuel, and I was in my working number eights. I was called to the gangway, and, when I arrived, there was Barbara waiting for me. The chap on the tanker said, "Come on – come and use my cabin. I will lock the door so nobody can interupt you."

Barbara and I had quite a long time in there. We didn't have sex or anything like that; we spoke of our love for each other and she said that once I finished with the navy I could go to California, where she came from and where her uncle was the commissioner of police, and her family would fit me up with a job.

I hurried back to the ship and arrived just as they were taking the gangway away. Jimmy, our first lieutenant, was waiting for me on the other side.

"That's the last time you will be seeing her, my boy," he said.

When we were back at sea the skipper announced over the Tannoy that we were not going to war; we were part of NATO's police, he said, but that turned out to be a load of old codswallop.

The very next morning, we were on the east coast of Korea. At five o'clock the klaxons went, and as we thought it was just a practice drill we just lay in our micks (hammocks). The next thing we knew, the old jaunty (ships policeman) and his accomplice, the RPO (regulating petty officer), came bashing us on the bottom of our micks with their batons. (That hurts!)

We all jumped out quick, because by now we could hear gunfire, and we rushed up to the upper deck. I was wearing just my underpants, a vest, and my anti-flash gear. This was absolutely stupid, because I had an unprotected body, a protected head and arms, and no protection on my legs. Why we wanted anti-flash gear I will never know! Six E-boats were coming out to attack us, and the *Juneau*, an American cruiser, which was ahead of us in line, had opened fire. She wasn't doing any damage, because all her shells were bursting above the boats, but our first salvo of six-inch shells dropped among them and split them all up. We were able to pick them off one by one.

The *Juneau* accounted for two: she sank one and the other beached and the crew escaped. We actually sank three of them. The sixth one went between us and the *Black Swan,* and the *Black Swan* gave chase, but whether or not she sunk the E-boat I do not know. It is unlikely that the *Black Swan* did catch it, because E-boats can do forty knots and the *Black Swan* could only do twenty at the most.

On another occasion, we had to go above the 38th parallel. We had heard that a Korean convoy was coming down the east coast, and we were ordered to destroy the road round the side of the mountain so that they couldn't get by.

Well, the *Juneau* said, "Leave it to us," but their shells landed well above the road.

They weren't getting the job done, so our skipper said, "Right, let's have a go," and after a couple of salvoes from our six-inch guns we blew the road to pieces.

We were cruising in convoy with the *Juneau* in front, the *Jamaica* and the *Black Swan* following, and we arrived at a bay with a big wooded area at the back of it.

The *Juneau* went well into the bay and nothing – absolutely nothing – happened, so we followed. Suddenly the guns from the shore opened up, and one of their shells caught our after mast. There were several casualties.

At the time we were carrying some soldiers, and I think they accounted for most of the dead. One of the AA gunners on the starboard side was also killed.

The skipper ordered the ship 'hard a-starboard' and 'full speed ahead' and we were out of range of the short guns in no time. We just sat back, out of range, and replied with our four- and six-inch guns. Every time we saw the red pinpricks of light as their guns fired from the shore, we would report to the bridge; the bridge would then report to the officers, and our guns would fire. We dealt with them quite well, but it was at the cost of those lives.

We were always popping up in different places, causing a bit of havoc. As a result, we became known as the *Phantom*.

In the meantime, the commies claimed that we, the ship HMS *Jamaica*, had been sunk, and when it was reported in the newspapers back in Japan my name was included among the dead. Poor old BG was in a bit of a stew.

When we got back to Sasebo, where our base was, I called BG up and she was overjoyed to hear we were all safe and sound. I don't know how they got hold of my name, or those of any of the others they listed as dead.

Some American marines came on board in Japan. They and some of our own marines had been assigned to make a landing above the 38th parallel to destroy a large power station.

They were supposed to make a landing at three o'clock in the morning, and, when the time came, we didn't hear a sound on board ship until the Americans came up on deck. Oh, they did make a noise! I don't know why they can't do things quietly.

Anyway, the skipper said, "It's all right, you boys. You can go and get your heads back down; our marines have already been and done the job." We never lost one man, and nobody heard a sound from them when they disembarked. This just shows you the difference between how we conducted ourselves in these kinds of actions and the way that the Americans did. I am sorry to say this – and it won't do a lot of good, will it? – but the Americans were so noisy! Sound carries further at night than it does during the day, so we had to be doubly careful, and that's why the skipper made the decision that he did.

We were always involved in some kind of action whilst we were cruising in Korean waters, and each time we went back to Sasebo for our short break to refuel and so on.

On one occasion, we were up the west coast. We were on our own there – there was no *Black Swan* and no *Juneau*. We were going very carefully because mines had been sighted. We were above the 38th parallel again, and we were the first ship of any of the navies there to negotiate these minefields. We had to keep our eyes peeled, day and night. As soon as a mine was spotted, the marines would come with their guns. It was a bit of practice for them, and they either sank it or blew it up. When I was on the watch, it always fell to me to go up into the eyes of the ship, which is right up in the sharp end, and keep a lookout for anything in the water. It was a very difficult job at night. We had a telephone, but by the time I had rung through to the bridge, the bloody thing could have hit us, couldn't it? Therefore, I never used the phone. I had a good strong voice, and as soon as I spotted something I used to cup my hands and shout up to the bridge, "Object, bearing green one O" or "green one five" or "green O five" or "red O five" or wherever it was. Then the searchlight would be directed on to it.

Sometimes it was an old oil drum or something, and sometimes it turned out to be a mine. If it was pretty well ahead, they were able to manoeuvre to avoid it, and they could sink it. I think I was sent up into the eyes of the ship more than anyone else because of the way I did it without resorting to the telephone. It was a more efficient method. Anyway, we negotiated the minefields many times before the war was over and never got damaged. We sunk a few and lived to tell the story.

Our marines had to make a landing on the west coast – I don't know what for this time, but we had to land them in the boats. I was one of the people chosen to hold the shore to make sure they would not get cut off. Fortunately, they came back after a successful operation, and there were no casualties. Nobody threatened us, so we all got back into the boats in an orderly fashion and arrived safely back on board.

On another occasion, we were not going very fast (somewhere around about seven knots or so), and suddenly the lookout shouted, "Object in the water!" As we moved closer, we could see bodies tied together. One of our boats went out to try to recover the bodies, but they had been in the water for a long time and the flesh just peeled away. The bodies had been tied in threes with their hands behind their backs, and each of them had a bullet wound in the back of the head. I suppose the North Koreans were responsible. None of the bodies were brought back on board; they were just left there to float about, and we carried on our way.

Suddenly, one night, the radar picked up a ship, and we asked it to identify itself with the code. We didn't get a reply, so we set sail after it. All night we pursued it down the coast towards South Korea, and on several occasions the skipper threatened to open fire if they didn't acknowledge our signal. We received no reply. When morning came, we saw that it was an American destroyer, and you should have heard the language our skipper used when he spoke to the skipper of the American destroyer. They had taken us away from our station, and we had wasted the whole night pursuing them.

On another occasion, the *Mighty Mo*, USS *Missouri*, the big battleship, asked us to identify ourselves or she would blow us out of the water.

At the time, we were taking on ammunition from an ammunition lighter off South Korea. The lighter was between us and the *Missouri*, and at the mast we were flying the red flag – red for danger. When we received the threat from the *Missouri*, our skipper was furious. With the ammunition lighter nearby, one shell could have blown the whole lot of us to smithereens. Just imagine it! The Americans' impetuousness, and their apparent inability to tell our flags and those of the communists apart, could have been disastrous.

After that we carried on patrolling in our normal fashion, but most of the time was uneventful.

We used to be piped over the side to go for a swim. All those ratings who wanted to swim did so, and it was a great challenge to see if anyone could swim under the ship from one side to the other. Very few people could do it, and I was able to earn myself some money by performing the feat. It was surprising how quickly I reached the bottom of the ship and went under the keel. Mind you, I have always had good lungs; I could swim the whole length of the swimming baths underwater. As I started coming up the other side of the ship, I had to remember to keep swimming outwards and not to come up too fast; on one or two occasions I caught my back on the ship's bottom, and it made me bleed. It hurt a bit too. As I swam upwards it would grow lighter and lighter and lighter and then suddenly I would break the surface.

One time I thought I wasn't going to make it, but I came up safely in the end. I heard all the blokes shouting, "There he is! There he is!" and so on. On that occasion, I picked up a fiver, which in those days was almost a month's wages for me. The skipper would throw grenades over the side to make sure the waters were safe for us to swim in, and a boat would go round picking up the dead or stunned fish for our meal. They made a very tasty change.

People did call me a mad bastard, so perhaps I was. I certainly used to do things that other people wouldn't do!

On another occasion the skipper wanted the underside of the crow's nest painted. Now, the crow's nest on a cruiser is perhaps seventy or eighty feet above the deck.

Dusty, the chief buffer, came up to me and said, "Hank, you are a mad bastard. Why don't you volunteer?" (He didn't say Heckford; he called me Hank. Everybody called me Hank – I don't know why.)

It was the topman's job really, and I was the fo'c's'le man, but as no one else would do it. I said, "All right, but it will cost you your tot."

I selected old Simo, my mate, as my stage manager, because I had to have somebody reliable there with me. Then up we went.

The sea was rough that day, and the ship swayed crazily from one side to the other, but we stayed up there all morning.

By lunchtime I had finished the job, so I went to the chief petty officer's mess to claim my tot.

When Dusty came to the door, I said, "Righto, Dusty, I have finished."

He said, "I should bloody well think so! You have been up there all morning."

I said, "Well, I gave it two coats. It won't need doing again now before we get back."

He went back into the mess, and came out with his tot of rum, which was about twice as much as you would get from an optic in a pub. He handed it to me, and I just saw the whole lot off.

He said, "You rotten bastard! You could at least have saved me a wet."

But I thought, 'No. I did the job so I take the rum!'

When anyone reached the age of twenty-one, he was given drinks by everyone on the mess deck. It was a recognised thing. Well, when it was my twenty-first birthday, I missed all my wets because I was on the MFV at Hong Kong. Therefore I had the celebrations on my twenty-second birthday instead.

By this time we were in Sasebo again, after doing a stint up the Korean coast.

I went round to all the messes when the tots were issued and had a wet from each man. When I got back to my own mess, I drank my own tot as well as a share of everyone else's. They told me I stayed on my feet for about an hour, but eventually I collapsed, so they put me on a camp bed under a table, out of harm's way.

Well, that was the idea. When I came to, at about

half past four, or five o'clock, I'd got a big plaster across the bridge of my nose. At first I thought somebody had been thumping me, but it turned out that Able Seaman Morely, the meteorological lad, had accidentally knocked away the support for the hinged portion of the table, which had swung down and caught me across my nose.

Anyway, I still went ashore that night, but I could only manage one or two drinks before I was gone again. The others had to carry me back on board. That was my twenty-second birthday – celebrated in great, traditional naval style.

I never contacted BG during this short spell in Sasebo. We had to sail back to Korea because a major operation was imminent. That was the Inchon Landings, in which we played a major part. We anchored in Inchon Harbour with hundreds of other ships – troopships and battleships and goodness knows what. Fairly close to us was an American cruiser.

I was assigned to F gun deck and F2 pom-pom. My job was to keep that part of the ship clean and to make sure the gun was always in tip-top condition. I had no other duties but this, and I always made sure the gun worked perfectly and was ready for action.

Our job was to bombard the area in preparation for the landings, and an American spotter plane was doing the spotting for us.

One of our salvoes hit an ammunition dump

almost twelve miles inland and blew the whole lot sky high. We could see the smoke from the explosion from aboard our ship. It went way up into the air. The American spotter was so excited that he forgot what he was there for. Our skipper said, "For God's sake, man, stop your gibbering and get on with your work!" It all came over the Tannoy, so we all heard it.

HMS *Jamaica* had done it again! We had quite a reputation for accurate gunnery.

At five o'clock one morning two aircraft were circling the ships in the harbour, and I said to George Ralph, the captain of the gun, "They are Yaks."

He said, "Are you sure?"

I said, "I'm absolutely sure." I had done aircraft recognition the night before, and I was absolutely certain of them. I said to the wireless operator attached to my gun, "Contact the bridge and tell them there are two Yaks circling."

The officer on watch said to the operator, "Don't be stupid – they are from the Australian carrier."

I said to George Ralph, "They are Yaks."

The aircraft came round for the second time and headed towards the cruiser next to us, which happened to be Admiral Struble's ship, and as soon as I heard the first bomb whistle down I opened fire. I am pretty certain I winged him, or at least injured the pilot, but the second aircraft was coming in so I automatically directed my gun towards him. I opened fire and put him off his aim, so only a crane at the back of the cruiser was damaged, but then he swung round and came towards the *Jamaica,* firing at us as he came. Mine was the only gun returning fire.

He hit my gun and Godsell, one of my ammunition loaders was so badly injured that he later died, but I immediately returned fire and blew him out of the sky.

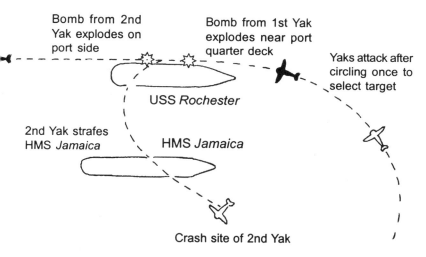

Bomb from 2nd
Yak explodes on
port side

Bomb from 1st Yak
explodes near port
quarter deck

Yaks attack after
circling once to
select target

USS *Rochester*

2nd Yak strafes
HMS *Jamaica*

HMS *Jamaica*

Crash site of 2nd Yak

The attack on USS Rochester *and HMS* Jamaica.

Godsell was only a young lad. He had only been an ordinary seaman for about three weeks and he had been put in the same mess as myself, so I was very sad when he died.

I got a bollocking for opening fire without permission; the other gun crews got a bollocking because they didn't open fire. All they recovered from that plane was one wheel. Later that day,

Admiral Struble came on board and praised the captain for his sharpshooting. The officers were all in bed at the time, but Admiral Struble gave our captain a bronze medal for the action, and I got a bollocking. I don't think it ever came to light that the officer of the watch was responsible for the plane getting round the second time. He could have opened fire and got them on the starboard side before they had circled the second time.

Later on, the skipper offered me a chance of promotion, but I turned it down on principle.

That was the first time I was offered promotion. The second time he sent his personal writer down to the mess deck to tell me I could go back to Guz to do the leading seaman's course. A month or so afterwards, I could put in for a petty officer's course and from then I could have become a chief or warrant officer. However, I still turned it down because of the principle of the thing. I had saved the ship and accounted for two enemy planes, and yet I had been told off.

Frank Goldsworthy, the war correspondent for the *Daily Express* interviewed me straight after the action, but all that went in the paper was that I had given a four-second burst and shot the plane down. A plane was found crashed in the hills a bit later and I am pretty certain it was the plane I had winged.

My photo was in the *Daily Express* and the *Daily Mirror*. When a reporter from the local paper went to see my mother, and said he'd come to see her about her son, she nearly fainted because she thought I had been killed. The engagement was also reported in the *Maltese Times*.

I have still got the cuttings. Most of the information came from someone who knew nothing about that action, and it is hopelessly inaccurate, but I am glad to be able to set the record straight at last.

John Oakley, able seaman on F1 pom-pom, which was a single barrel, was as mad as hell because he couldn't open fire. His gun was stripped down and the parts were all over the deck. He was fuming because he had a misfire.

My target selection officer, an RPO, was always telling us how brave he had been during the war, but when the action started he had jumped underneath the mounting. That's how brave he was.

An Australian was in the director beside my gun. He said, "I always thought us Australians were mad bastards, but you beat us to that one. You are the maddest bastard I have ever come across."

I had to fight the entire action off my own back, without support, and it was because I did things like this that I was called a mad bastard.

Apart from young Godsell, there were two more ammunition runners – a couple of boy seamen. Their job was to collect the ammunition from the ammunition locker, run it over to my gun and hand it to my two ammunition loaders. However, they too dived for cover. There was a bunker close by, but their legs stuck out and they both got slightly injured by shrapnel.

Recently, someone has put on the Internet that all guns on the ship were firing. The writer was, at the time, a boy seaman on the *Jamaica* and he wasn't even on the upper deck. He reports that Admiral Brown had warned us that enemy aircraft were approaching. Absolute rubbish! There was no warning of these planes whatsoever. If there had been, they wouldn't have got that far. What I have told you in this account is the true report of that action.

The only officer that wasn't in bed at the time (the duty officer) told my wireless operator they were Australian aircraft, which proves we were never forewarned.

The only firing came from my gun, although the marines did get a few shots off after the whole thing was over. The only correct information in the Internet account is that young Godsell was killed, but he wasn't a boy seaman. He had been an ordinary seaman since about three weeks before, when he was placed in the same mess as I was.

Life is a funny old thing really. I thoroughly enjoyed my life in the navy and I grew to really love it, but in some ways I regret not taking promotion when it was offered.

While we were at Inchon, we weren't far from the shore when suddenly a machine gun opened fire at us from a barn in a field adjacent to the harbour. We were ordered to return fire. As it was such close range, I had to use the old-fashioned cross-wire sights, which are difficult to use accurately. It was no good trying to use the gyro at that range.

Anyway, a couple of rounds went into the barn, so the commies came out and ran across the field towards the woodland. I continued firing, and I could see my shells landing among them. A couple of them dropped, but the rest made it to the wood.

I felt satisfied that we had done a difficult job well, but, as on many other occasions, we felt that our efforts were not properly recognised.

We were a hell of a long time in Inchon, but most of us were just onlookers. When the big guns opened fire, we watched the results, and it was very, very exhilarating.

The Inchon Landings went quite smoothly, without a great loss of life, and I like to think we contributed to the success of the operation.

I think the landings at Inchon must have been one of the biggest since the end of the Second World War. It was unbelievable how many ships were packed in that harbour. Not very much was ever reported about the Korean War; even now you don't hear much about it, which is rather surprising because it was quite a bloody and nasty war. We lost quite a lot of men there, and so did America and other countries as well.

After the landings, we resumed our normal

patrols up the east and west coasts of Korea, with occasional trips back to Sasebo in Japan.

CHAPTER 9: Hong Kong

After the war had ended, we never went back to Sasebo. We went to Hong Kong, where we had a couple of months to get over what we had been through – which wasn't a lot really. To be perfectly honest, I enjoyed the conflict. I suppose that is not the right thing to say, but it's how I felt. It was what I joined the navy for.

In Hong Kong, we were given shore leave, and I was walking towards the Fleet Club, near Wan Chai, when I recognised a blond-headed matelot who was walking towards me. It was Frankie Lane, and we had been at school together many years before.

Suddenly, all that distance away from our home country, there he was, walking up the road in Hong Kong.

On the same day as I met Frankie Lane, I also bumped into some friends of BG's from the Women's Royal Australian Army Corps (WRAAC). I hadn't been in touch with her, and again she thought I had been killed. "You rotten bastard!" one of them said. "Poor BG has been crying her eyes out. I am going to write and tell her that I have seen you, so she will know what a rotten sod you are."

I decided, there and then, that it was best to let things go. She would be going back to America; I was going back to Guz, England. So there wasn't a lot of future there, was there? I decided not to correspond with her any further, and the episode was over and done with.

When we left the theatre of war, my job changed. I became what they call 'Tanky', which meant I was in charge of the issue room. I had six chaps under me, so it was like a small promotion really, although I was still an able seaman. We had to supply all the food for all the meals for the crew, including a light tea (jam, sugar, butter, milk, etc.) at about four o'clock. It was my job, right up until I left the ship, to see that every mess got its exact quota of issues.

I had to adapt quickly from being a gun sweeper, looking after a gun, to being in charge of the issue room.

The butcher and I had to measure out the rum in front of the officer of the watch, and the rum was then watered down to make grog in a big rum barrel. Each rating had almost half a pint of grog, a third of which was neat rum. It was very strong indeed, and it was well worth having. We called it gibbering juice, because once every rating had had their tots, everybody started talking at once. I suppose you might compare us to a load of old women really, once we had all had our tots.

One chap in our mess was an old-timer and a bit of a wag. He was a special-sea-duty man, and if he got piped to his quarters, he would always take out his false teeth and put them in his issue of rum until he came back. That way, he knew damn well that no one was going to drink his tot while he was gone.

In Hong Kong, Ted, Simo, Johnny Michaels and I went over to a bar in Kowloon. After a few glasses of the old Tiger beer, I got a bit merry and decided I wanted to be a javelin thrower. It was all high spirits. I got hold of an old mop, shouted at everybody, "Stand clear! Here comes the champion javelin thrower," and I threw this old mop across a couple of the tables. I didn't mean to cause trouble, but a few glasses were knocked over, and the next minute about a dozen Chinese people came from the back of the bar, yelling and carrying truncheons.

We all ran like hell into the street and up a side road. There was a high wall at the end, and we thought we were trapped, but a narrow passage led through to another road. When we were on the other side, running along the road, I suddenly shouted out, "Where's Johnny Michaels, then?" and a voice replied from down below. He was running along a trench, and I could just see his blond head bobbing up and down.

The Chinese gave up the chase, but we had to pass the bar again on the way back to the ship. We just walked by, calmly and quietly, and nothing at all happened.

About 250 of us entered a foot race around Hong Kong, but on the way I met my mates and I stopped at a pub for a beer or two. I still came twenty-seventh, which wasn't bad, considering.

While I was in the navy my highest position in a foot race was fifth out of more than 500 people. I did very well on that one, but I had no stoppages on the way. I just ran. I used to love running and walking.

While we were in Hong Kong, a young married chap from our ship was murdered. He went ashore on his own, which is something you shouldn't do, and that night he didn't return. At first he was reported absent without leave, but then his body was found. He had been stabbed. He was a keen photographer, and it was thought that he had been killed for his camera. When somebody died we held what they call a 'sale at the mast'. All the dead man's belongings were sold and the money was sent to his next of kin, which in this case was his wife. It was very sad.

We were warned that a hurricane was going to hit Hong Kong, and every ship had to leave the harbour. All the merchant ships, warships and so on put out to sea. Believe me, it was rough! The ship went down so fast into the trough of a wave that our feet actually left the deck and met the ship as it was coming back up again. It was terrific, and yet I enjoyed every moment of it. It was great. A lot of the lads were sick, which meant I had an extra tot of rum or so – which went down very well.

Once it had calmed down a bit, we saw a junk that had lost all its sails. Another one had been broken in half, so we rescued the people from that one and towed the other junk all the way back to Hong Kong. A merchant ship that hadn't made it out to sea had been swept on to the jetty by the force of the storm. I don't know how they got it back into the water, because it was still there when we sailed for England soon afterwards.

On our way back to England we stopped for a couple of days at Ceylon, which is now called Sri Lanka. Whilst we were there, we had an SOS to say that the troopship *Devonshire* was adrift in the Bay of Biscay. We set sail at top speed, but then we heard that she was under steam again. When we got to the Suez Canal, we, being a warship, had priority and any other ship had to gare up for us. We were about three-quarters of the way through when we were told that the *Devonshire* was ahead of us, waiting for us to go by. She was taking British troops to Malaya. As we passed, everybody was yelling and waving their hats, and one man in particular was up on the boat davits, yelling and waving his hat: "Heckford! Heckford! Heckford!" It was my younger brother, Wilfred.

I shouted back, but he never saw me among all the other matelots.

I didn't know he was aboard until I heard him calling my name and saw him waving his hat like mad.

We stopped in Malta for a few days, and the exploits of HMS *Jamaica* were reported in the Maltese newspapers. Not everything was correct, but it wasn't far out.

CHAPTER 10: Devonport

We got back to Guz early one morning. It was winter time and it was very cold and frosty. It wasn't a very nice welcome to come back on that cold, dark English morning – from warm to cold, just like that!

When we returned, we called in at Weymouth for about three days.

When my friends came back from a night ashore, one of them said, "Hank, if I were you, I wouldn't go ashore." He said there was a young lady on the jetty waiting for me with a child.

It must have been the girl I met there before we sailed for the West Indies, but I didn't go ashore. I reasoned that if I had got together with her that quickly, then so could somebody else; I could never be sure that it was my kiddie. I never saw her and I never saw the child, but apparently it was a little boy. In one way I am glad I did not see them, but in another way I am a bit sorry. Perhaps it was my son.

Whilst we were in dry dock at Devonport, we had

to use the shore heads. One day four or five people were playing poker, and one of them was reluctant to leave the table to go to the heads because he kept winning, hand after hand.

I said to him after a while, "If you don't soon go, mate, you are going to shit yourself."

He said, "Well, how can I go when I keep getting hands like this?"

Suddenly he stood up, put his cards down on the table and said, "Don't let anybody see those cards, Hank." Then he minced his way across the deck. We all watched as he went up the ladder, over the combing and across the fo'c's'le. He was more than halfway across the gangway when suddenly the back part of his trousers just burst. He had shit himself.

A great cheer went up, but instead of carrying on over to the heads, he came back, sat down, picked his hand up and won the round. He picked the money up and then he shot off to clean himself up.

We played all kinds of card games, and we made our own amusements. We were never really bored even when we were at sea for very long spells at a time. I didn't get involved with too many sports or games because I liked to read. I would take a book and tuck myself away in a corner of the mess or on the upper deck.

I also took up carpentry. Instead of going ashore with my mates, I had woodwork lessons with the CPO carpenter. I made a round coffee table, which

I still have. It was made from the top of the captain's old mahogany desk, so I still have a little bit of the *Jamaica* with me even now.

When I got the coffee table completed, I had a weekend leave, and I decided to take it with me to Chorleywood. I also took a standard lamp I had made. However, no matter how I twisted and turned it, the coffee table would not go through the doorway of the carriage. In the end, the guard said, "Shove it in here. Come on!" and he dragged me into the guard's van with him. I had to stay there all the way up to London.

Then, I had to go on the Tube to Baker Street. The standard lamp was six foot tall so progress was difficult. Two or three people gave me a helping hand, but I still knocked into at least two people as I got on the Tube. At Baker Street I went straight to the guard's van and stayed there until the train reached Chorleywood. A local taxi took me the rest of the way. It took quite a bit of trouble, but it is a nice coffee table and I had to get it home somehow.

We all had a fair amount of leave to come, and on the first leave I went home.

On my second leave I met my wife at a dance. Audrey was her name. She didn't want to dance with me at first, because I was a little bit wild on the floor. She had a bad ankle where she had scalded it with hot water from a kettle, and I think she was frightened that I might give it a good knock. Anyway, I eventually persuaded her to dance and

I was careful not to knock her ankle. I ended up taking her home.

I had one more leave whilst we were still in Devonport, and I spent most of that leave with Audie, after a short spell at Southend with my aunt.

Our courtship was very short, because the *Jamaica* sailed up to Rosyth in Scotland. I had a long trip to Devonport during my Christmas leave, but I was back in Scotland for Hogmanay. I had a whale of a time.

Old Dickie Baird said, "You come with me," so I did. We started off with a bottle of whisky, then we got welcomed at the first house (drinks all round), then we went to another house (again drinks all round), and so on. Whenever we went from one house to another we always had a bottle, but it was always a different bottle. We had a wonderful, wonderful time that Hogmanay.

We got back on board eventually – in a none-too-healthy state, I may add.

After that I put in for a long weekend, travelled down to home to see Audie, and proposed to her. She accepted and we married on 14 April 1952, when I had a fortnight's leave.

Before marriage, Audrey and I were together for only about five weeks, and we were married for fifty-four years. A hell of a lot of people said that it wouldn't last, but it did.

We couldn't have a proper honeymoon. Our honeymoon was spent in her parents' house and then I had to return to the *Jamaica* up in Scotland.

At about this time, the butcher and I worked out a device so we could get the rum to drip from the breaker in which it was kept. Hour after hour it used to drip, drip into the big measure, until there was enough for a decent drink.

Another of our tricks was to put a finger in the top of the measure as we were issuing the rum. Each time we did that we saved a fingertip full of rum for ourselves.

Once I became 'Tanky' I had access to more rum than was good for me really, I think.

On the *Jamaica*, we had some entertainment from time to time. In the topman's mess there was a young chap who was a bit of a hypnotist, and I was invited in to watch him perform a couple of times. He put some of the chaps under the old spell, so to speak, and he got them to do rather silly things. He got one of them to act like a woman, and he told another of the lads to behave as if the first chap was his wife.

I would still like to know if we were the only ship ever to join in a guard of honour at Edinburgh Castle. The Sutherland Highlanders, the RAF and the Royal Marines were also involved.

We were very, very proud of ourselves doing this guard of honour. Photographers from the local papers were there to take pictures, and one of them nipped in front of us and fell over. We just marched over him, and none of us went out of step.

I heard that volunteers were needed back in Guz to get HMS *Warrior* ready for commissioning, so I put my name forward and in two or three weeks I was on my way back to Devon with about 200 others.

When the train reached London, I caught another train to Chorleywood and spent a few short, happy hours with Audie before dashing back to London to catch the night train to Devonport.

CHAPTER 11: HMS *Warrior*

The *Warrior* was an aircraft carrier, and I was made 'Tanky'. We had nowhere near a full crew; we were just there to keep the ship clean and ready for commissioning. Fortunately, I was able to spend quite a few weekends with Audie.

One of the crew members on the *Warrior* went missing for several days. He was posted absent without leave, and nobody could trace him.

One day the naval shore patrol in Plymouth saw some women behaving suspiciously, so they followed them to where they lived, and there they found the missing sailor. Apparently, the women had enticed him into their place when he went ashore and they kept him a prisoner there. He would never discuss what they did to him, but it must have been an ordeal because he didn't look much of a lad after he had got back on board ship. He never got charged with being absent without leave, because he was kept under duress. The women were very funny people, from what we gathered.

When Audie was expecting our first child, I was

given compassionate leave, and as the baby was overdue I applied for some extra days. In those days, babies were often born at home, but eventually Audie was taken into hospital. My extra leave expired, but the doctor wouldn't give me a note to get it extended again. Nevertheless I overstayed my leave by another week. Three weeks altogether went by, and she still hadn't had the baby, so I just had to go back on board. I had been absent without permission for a week, but they were pretty fair with me: they just gave me a week's stoppage of leave and pay. I wasn't supposed to get my tot either, but, being 'Tanky', I could work it so I had one anyway.

After I had been back on board about three days, I got a telegram from my brother-in-law telling me all was well. 'A baby daughter. Daughter and mother doing very well.' There you are – that's how I became a dad.

One day, while I was still on the punishment, I gave a bit of a fright to one of the men. It was the same man as was kept prisoner by the women in Plymouth. We were going to have a cigarette in the empty hangar, and he said, "Here you are, Hank – here's a light." As I turned round, the little devil (he was always a bit of a joker) put the lighter up against my face so the flame went up my nose.

I grabbed hold of him and said, "Right, you are going through the porthole now."

I carried him over to the porthole and made out I was going to push him through. The other blokes said, "No, Hank, don't be stupid! Don't be stupid! Don't do that! Don't do that!"

They thought that I was cross enough to actually do it, but I was just getting a little bit of my own back, and giving him a fright. God! it was a dry dock, so, if I had pushed him through it would have killed the poor lad.

I put him down and said, "Right, don't you ever do that again, because next time I *will* push you through."

I didn't mean that either. We were old mates off the *Jamaica*, and we generally all had a good laugh together.

Going back to the *Jamaica*, when we returned to Guz we found out that one of the young lads had never had scrumpy in his life, so on his twenty-first birthday my mates and I took him ashore for some real, rough farm cider. We only had a few bob, but it was only about eight pence a pint.

After one pint, this lad was pretty well gone, and after we had also had our fill we got him back on board. We slung his hammock, then took his top and trousers off and heaved him in. He slept well all night.

Well, the next morning, reveille sounded and as he was a former boy seaman he was used to getting up straight away, but he was unprepared for the effect of the scrumpy. If you aren't used to it, scrumpy can run through you like water, and as he swung his legs over the edge of the hammock it just shot straight out. He never got a drop on himself; it just went straight out and over the deck. The smell was terrible, and the poor lad had a hell of a lot of cleaning up to do – but he did it, I will give him that.

He never ever touched scrumpy again, and he wouldn't speak to me or my mates for ages afterwards. As far as he was concerned, we were entirely to blame.

In those days, there were well over 100 blokes on our mess desk alone, so there was very little space. Nowadays they've got bunks, and they don't know what it's like to have to sling a hammock. The hammock had to be packed away tight and firm during the day. It had seven rings, and each had to be pulled in taut. If a ship was hit below the waterline, the hammocks could be used to bung the holes up, to stop the water flooding in, but if they were loosely packed, they wouldn't do the job. Water would seep through. Therefore, there were hammock inspections – and God help the person who didn't do his hammock up properly! He would have to sling it and pack it away repeatedly until the officer was satisfied. It was discipline, and we had plenty of that.

Soon after Marilyn was born, Audie brought her down to live with me in a flat in Devonport, right opposite the barrack gates. All I had to do was just walk through the barrack gates, cross the road and I was home.

I always managed to take something home with me, like butter, sugar and jam. All those things were still rationed, but, being 'Tanky', I could get hold of them. I always covered my tracks, and I always made sure the paperwork showed nothing was missing. I would give the old butcher some butter, and in return he would give me a fillet steak – a full fillet! – which I wrapped in greaseproof paper around my tummy. Then I could walk out across the dockyard, through the barracks and out through the barrack gates. The petty officer on watch was an ex-shipmate from the *Dunkirk*, so he just used to wave me through. When I got home, my underclothes were covered in blood, but it was lovely fillet steak. It was brilliant.

The only time I couldn't go across and see my wife and my little daughter was when we put to sea for a day or two. They were happy there. The people who owned the flat lived below, and they were very, very nice people. They looked after Audrey and Marilyn whilst I was at sea, so I never had any worries there.

Gradually we got a full crew on the *Warrior*. A new catapult for catapulting off aircraft was installed on board. It was a new type of steam catapult. I think I am right in this, but I was only a seaman, and I had very little to do with the aircraft or flight deck. When they were testing the catapult, they used to fire a 2-ton block of wood across the basin. This went on for weeks, until they got the tension right and they could reach the other side of the basin. The block used to splash down into the water, then they would recover it, bring it back on board, adjust the catapult and then try it again.

By the time the catapult was working perfectly, we had taken on a full crew. I had about eleven blokes under me in the issue room, and we had to keep the crew fed, as we did on the *Jamaica*, including sorting out the rum rations.

Then we put to sea and found out what it was like to land a jet on board ship, which had never been done before. The jet was launched into the air successfully and landed several times; then we went back into harbour, where a few more adjustments were made.

When we put to sea again, two jets landed on the deck, one behind the other. They were caught with the arrester wires, and then they were launched with the catapult, one after the other.

HMS *Warrior* was the first aircraft carrier to land and launch jets at sea.

After being on the *Warrior* for, I suppose, almost a year, I was demobbed on 7 May 1954. Captain Stores came down for me personally, and he said I had been such a good chap that he never had to query any of my white sheets. He said there were never any mistakes whatsoever, and I was by far the best 'Tanky' that had ever served under him. He asked me to sign on to stay in the Andrew (the Royal Navy) and become his personal 'Tanky', so that whichever ship he went on I would go with him.

However, by now my wife and I had a little baby girl, and they were living right opposite the barrack gates in Devonport. I told the Captain that Audie was adamant that she wanted me to leave the navy, and he asked me if I would mind him going to have a chat with her.

I said, "Well, you can, but I can tell you the answer now: she wants me to leave."

When the Captain came back on board, he said, "You are absolutely right, and I agree with what she says."

He couldn't persuade her, so that was that. I got my demob, but it wasn't a bed of roses, because I found it hard to settle down in civilian life.

CHAPTER 12: Civilian Life

I really did love the navy. The navy was my life, but I had to make a choice and in the end my family was more important.

After I had left the navy, I was on five years' reserve. I had to go back for a week, and during that week I had to do some polishing-up and training on my gunnery. Things had advanced a bit since I last fired the guns, but the target plane came and it was my turn to fire.

I opened fire, and with a short burst I shot the drogue down, but the officer in charge was not pleased.

"You silly sod!" he said. "You are not supposed to shoot it down; you are supposed to aim close to it."

I said, "What's the bloody good of aiming close to it? If it's a proper target, you have to shoot it down, and that's what I have done."

I was not very popular that time.

On the last day we were there, we were given mock ammunition – Bakelite shells, which splintered when they left the muzzle of the gun. We were supposed to stop firing, but the jets came roaring in so low that I couldn't resist.

One of the pilots said, "We are not bloody well coming back there with them mad bastards!"

I had splintered one of their fuselages with a load of the Bakelite! I always aimed to shoot down, not to miss, but on some occasions it didn't make me very popular. I still enjoyed firing the guns. That was one of my great joys in the navy. I used to love it.

I couldn't get a job that I wanted, so I ended up training as a slaughter man. I became quite an efficient chap at that. I used to do all the killing.

The Jewish slaughter men came every Wednesday to kill their calves, and one time I decided to give them a shock. One of the lads had brought in a starting pistol, so I loaded it with blanks and dashed into the room where the Jews were.

"Right, you bastards!" I shouted. "This is for coming here and stealing our work." Then I started firing the blanks, and they started ducking and diving. It must have been pretty frightening for them, but I was just having a mad skylark. As I told you before, when I was in the navy I was always called a mad bastard!

It was very, very heavy work, and after nine or ten years it kind of got the better of me, so I packed it in and got another job. That didn't last long, so I tried to go back into the navy. I think I was thirty-two at the time, and I was two years over the five years' reserve, so they wouldn't take me back in.

I went from a job to a job to a job to a job, and finally I was taken on in a boiler-making factory. In time I became the shop foreman there, but I missed the navy. The navy was still in my blood.

The Andrew made me a very versatile person, and one thing I became good at was York-stone splitting. I think I became quite professional at it. I did a lot of York-stone splitting for a friend of mine who had his own business.

Along my way I have made some good friends among people that I have worked for, and two such friends are Richard and Trish Sankey. I hold them in great esteem. They are the type of people you might call a lady and gentleman. They have three daughters – Tina, Amanda and Jo – I watched them grow up. It is wonderful to know that I have their friendship.

Gill and Rob are another great couple. I keep promising to visit them, but something always happens to prevent me from going. I am looking forward to walking in their garden with them. I know that if I go up there to see them, they will make a fuss of me, because they are very nice people.

I have joined the British Legion and the Royal Naval Association (RNA), and there I have met some good shipmates. We call ourselves shipmates, because that's what we are.

I have a fair old laugh with Dave Pearson, the chairman of our RNA branch. He was in the navy for longer than I was, but I joined up before he did. We have a get-together, and we sit down and recount our stories and our times in the old Andrew. Being ex-matelots, we are somehow very different to ordinary civilians, or even the army boys. We ex-matelots are like one big family really. We have all experienced similar things and we are all drawn to ships and the seafaring life. I would have loved to spend longer in the navy.

Brian Brown is a life member of the RNA now, and he was one of the founder members of the Chesham branch of the Sea Cadets. He has quite a lot to do with them on and off, and we are sometimes invited to join in their dos too. We have one or two little drinks and a meal, and a pleasant evening is had by all.

We also have other dos with other branches of the RNA. We get invited out to them, and we invite them back to our place, and we all have a good time. Everybody gets together, everybody enjoys themselves, and that's what it is all about.

After losing my wife – God rest her soul! – I realised just how lonely life can be, so the RNA has become an important part of my life. Every Sunday lunchtime I go there, and I meet the lads at the British Legion and my other mates as well. It takes some of the loneliness away.

It is now coming up for two years since Audie died – bless her heart! – and now I have met a very special lady. Her name is Jean, and she is my next-door neighbour. We laugh and joke quite a lot, and she is excellent company. There is another lady as well: that's Edie. We get together and in the afternoons we go down into the lounge of the complex where I now live. There we sit and laugh and talk and read the papers. Life is now nowhere near as lonely as it was.

I should explain that after Audie died, on 13 September 2006, I couldn't live on my own in the bungalow any more. I applied for sheltered accommodation at Cromwell House, and that's where I am now.

With all the help and comradeship, I am now three times the man I was when I first came in here. I know I have got a lot wrong with me, including prostate cancer, but I just live for the day and I am really enjoying my life quite a lot.

In an emergency I can just pull a cord to summon help. Lynne Eckhart, the sheltered-housing officer, calls us every day to make sure we are OK.

When I moved into this sheltered accommodation I was in a very sad situation. I was grieving for my wife, and I was very ill. Lynne was great towards helping me recuperate, and, after a couple of months, Jean used to knock on my door to see if I was OK. It is thanks to Lynne and Jean that I am now as well as I am.

Jean is a great friend – a very dear friend.

Early one morning, I had a stroke. I couldn't use my hands, and all I could do was gurgle. My brain was working well enough, but I couldn't talk. I pulled the emergency cord, and within about four minutes the paramedics arrived.

That's what sheltered accommodation is all about. The paramedics sorted me out and got me to hospital. From then on it was recovery time. It wasn't a large stroke – thank goodness! After a couple of days I got all the movement back in my arms and legs. The only thing is, to this day I still have trouble in getting some of my words out. They have become a little bit rolled up, so to speak. However, on the whole I have recovered quite well.

My daughter, who works for the police at Tring, came and picked me up from the hospital when she had finished work one evening. I could not stay there another night, because it was quite unbearable in the ward that they put me in.

I can say this about living in Cromwell House: we do get some excitement. Every flat is fitted with a smoke alarm, and if somebody burns the toast or overcooks food, the smoke alarm goes off. Then everybody has to follow the fire drill and go outside, and the fire brigade comes racing in.

On one occasion we did have a big fire here. A chap in one of the flats dropped his cigarette into the waste bin by his chair, and it burst into flames. Luckily, the poor old boy had the sense to get out, so he wasn't hurt – thank goodness! – but it caused quite a stir. It was quite a fire!

The old fire brigade was here in no time, but it took them a fair bit of time to deal with it. The episode brought home to us how lucky we are to have people looking out for us.

We had another stir yesterday, as a matter of fact. A lady and a chap in the flat below Jean's were frying sausages and the fire alarms went off. We all had to evacuate our flats, and the only people who didn't come out were the people who caused the alarm to go off. They never had the decency to come out and apologise to everybody.

I have now had prostate cancer for eight years. The doctors have told me I won't die because of it, but I will die with it. I've been told that men who have their prostate gland removed can still perform sex-wise, but that doesn't matter at all to me.

I would like everyone to spare a thought for the brave seamen of Britain and the Commonwealth – in the merchant navy as well as the Royal navy – who have lost their lives fighting to keep this a free country for the rest of us.

If it hadn't have been for the navy and merchant navy in the last war, there would have been no Battle of Britain because there would have been no fuel for the planes. And if there had been no Battle of Britain, there would be no Britain left, would there? We would all now be under Nazi occupation. So just think about that for a little while, please.

Before I finish, I would like to thank the staff and doctors at Water Meadow Surgery in Chesham. All the reception staff are exceptional, wonderful people. They make sure everyone is seen quickly, and they and the doctors seem to really care about their patients. I am thinking particularly of an occasion when, although it was out of hours, the quick action of a receptionist and one of the doctors helped to save the lives of two of my dearest friends, both of whom are elderly.

It is a different kind of love when you get older; the love is entirely different from when you are younger. When you are younger, it's love and sex and so on, but as you get older it's love and respect for each other and that's what Audie and I had in plenty. God rest her soul.

Audrey and myself had two wonderful kids. They were never any bother, and they grew up to be the same – wonderful poeple. They look after their old dad quite well, and I thank them very much. I have got four lovely, lovely grandchildren. I shall be seeing them this Christmas.